RISING ABOVE

PARKINSON'S

*TAKE ON LIFE'S GREATEST CHALLENGES
AND LEARN TO THRIVE!*

GREG RITSCHER

DELPHI
PUBLISHING

GregRitscher.com

What readers are saying about

RISING ABOVE PARKINSON'S

"Packed with ... helpful information and tips, all based on the author's personal experience living with Parkinson's. I highly recommend this book!"
— **John M Dean, MA, CCC-SLP, Parkinson's Specialist,** *JohnMDean.com*

"Much more than a how-to book ...
It is a snapshot of a man who is truly loved and appreciated by the people around him both in sickness and in health."
— **Joe Miller, Chairman of the Board,** *Parkinson's Pointe*

"*Rising Above Parkinson's* is an upbeat read covering everything you need to know about Parkinson's Disease, with humor, faith, and a big dose of good-old-fashioned motivation!"
— *COMKAID Book Reviews*

"Those who apply the principles in this book will discover how adversity can be harnessed to realize the greatest meaning, purpose, and impact of our lives."
— **Dr. Wayne C. Darbonne, Pastor,** *St. James Presbyterian Church, Littleton, Colorado*

"An engaging book that will motivate readers to thrive despite their diagnosis."
— **Shari McMinn, author and speaker,** *sharimcminn.com*

Rising Above Parkinson's
Take on Life's Greatest Challenges and Learn to Thrive

ISBN: 979-8-6279-9995-1

Written by: Gregory B. Ritscher

Published by: Delphi Publishing,
Greg Ritscher, GregRitscher.com

Edited by: Shari Howard McMinn, ShariMcMinn.com

Designed by: COMKAID.com

Cover and interior Photographs: Nic Daughtry, NicDaughtry.com

Printed and sold by: Amazon.com and affiliate distributors

CONTENTS

DEDICATION

This book is dedicated to:

God, and His plan for my life
Phylis, the love of my life
My daughters and sons-in-law, the fruit of my life
My grandchildren, the crowns of my life
My friends and fellow travelers in our journey for significance.

ACKNOWLEDGEMENTS

I would like to acknowledge:

My fellow Parkinsonian pals,
I hope this book helps you rise to the challenge of your life to thrive.
I wish you strength and peace on your journey.

My grandchildren,
they are the reason I am writing this book.
I hope I leave them a legacy of wisdom to use in their lives, which helps
chart their course for the future.

Kim, Shari, Zane,
and all those who helped bring this book to fruition
through their thoughts and contributions.
I could not have done this without your support!

Above all, Phylis, my wife,
for her unwavering love, guidance, and devotion.
"For better or worse" are easy words to say
but much harder to live by.
You have surpassed them all!

FORWARD

March 2020

This book is a fresh take on life with Parkinson's from someone who knows how to leverage his support system and focus on the important things in life. Greg really takes time to "show his work", breaking down key concepts into digestible components and providing tools for applying some of the best elements of his mindset to your own experience. Packed within all of this perspective are helpful information and tips, all based on the author's personal experience living with Parkinson's.

Knowing Greg's professional background, it's very interesting to see how his business acumen and related skills have managed to apply to the way he is going about his life after his diagnosis. As someone who has clearly had to manage a number of people, as well as sell and interact with a wide range of clients, he faced his first "Atomic Event" with a unique set of skills that immediately caught my attention.

Although Greg quickly became ensconced in all of the right habits, including regular vigorous exercise and a focus on diet and sleep hygiene, I think just as important was his strong relationship with his family and his community, including his church.

About this time last year, I was doing user testing on a project with some people living with Parkinson's. I was working with a brilliant user experience specialist, Luke Waaler, who was donating his time and expertise to help our little startup. Greg came in near the end of the session and it quickly became clear that he and Greg knew each other. In fact, Greg and Luke were both mentoring for their church together when Luke first moved to Colorado a number of years ago. The two shared a couple of warm memories about that experience while Greg got ready to help us learn how to improve what we were building.

It was a nice little surprise that was actually not really that surprising given what I've come to know about Greg over the years. Here's a man that works hard at everything he does, whether it's at work, in his home or at his church. And he brings that same mindset to how he lives with his Parkinson's. Now he's put all of that work and all of those insights into the book you see before you. I hope you enjoy it as much as I did.

Take a look for yourself and see if he doesn't change your perspective about a thing or two. I highly recommend this book!

— John M. Dean, MA, CCC-SLP

INTRODUCTION - WHY ME?

I heard the words, "You have Parkinson's disease." on April 26th, 2011 at about 10:45am, at Swedish Medical Center, Denver, Colorado, in a 5th floor doctor's office facing south. Other than that, I do not remember much about the diagnosis. Ha, ha.

My first question was, "How will this affect my lifespan?" The doctor said that Parkinson's "tends" to shorten a person's life span, and the final years might not be very fun. With that, I began a long journey to finish my life strong, following God's plan, to become an example for my wife, children, grandchildren, and friends of what it means to have the "peace that passes all understanding"[1] in your heart.

Up to that point in my life, I had been a hard driving, "Type A", "Warlord of Commerce". Now, I was a 55-year-old diseased person that had to eat soup and shave with my left hand (I am right-handed and right-side tremored).

Murphy's Law, Kismet, bad karma ... it seems that every culture, religion, and nationality has a phrase for bad things that will happen at some time in your life. Some bad things are annoying or inconvenient; we might be able to ignore them or shake them off. Sometimes these bad things will even just sort themselves out over time. But, then there are those bad things that have the ability to truly devastate us, things that don't "just sort themselves out". I call those in the worst category "Atomic Events".

An Atomic Event is any event that creates a collision of forces in your normal life, that has potentially catastrophic impacts, over which you believe you have no control. You know it's Atomic when your once normal life will never be normal again! You must focus your efforts on harnessing this energy to create a new normal life, for the rest of your life. If the energy given off from the event is not harnessed properly, it will destroy — rather than empower — the recipient. Hearing that you have cancer,

---

[1] *And the peace of God, which transcends all understanding, will guard your hearts and your minds in Christ Jesus* (Phillipians 4:7).

finding out a loved one has died suddenly, or learning your spouse wants a divorce are all examples that slap you in the face with this new reality. They are Atomic Events.

I have been an avid reader all my life and I have amassed a number of business and philosophical models from various books. My Parkinson's diagnosis gave me an opportunity to implement them in a proactive manner. It has been a way to show myself that we humans truly do have "Response-Ability". This is a teaching from Victor Frankl[2], a psychologist who survived Auschwitz. He believed that human beings have the unique capacity to respond to a stimulus — good or bad — in any fashion we choose. We are not limited to a fight or flight response from a major threat stimulus such as an Atomic Event. We have the capacity to stop and choose our response to any problem that confronts us. I have learned that the ONLY thing you can control in your life is your attitude.

If I had the choice to get rid of Parkinson's Disease in my life, I would. But as you will discover while reading this book, many people think I am a better, kinder, and gentler person because of my Parkinson's. The Apostle Paul in his second letter to the Corinthians wrote of his desire to have his physical ailments (the "thorn in his flesh") removed by God. Paul heard from God that in his weakness he is in fact made stronger and able to live a more influential life by having to trust in God during his suffering. Likewise, Parkinson's has taught me that my weakness actually has the ability to make me a better person with a more meaningful life, if I am trusting in God through this difficult journey.

In each chapter, I will introduce the following elements:

- **MODEL** — To help you understand how to implement the major focus of that chapter. I have found that models help me to "see" the solutions to life's problems, better than if I just try to think my way out of the problem. Albert Einstein is quoted as saying "We cannot solve our problems with the same thinking we used when we created them."[3]

[2] Frankl, Victor E., *Man's Search for Meaning,* 1946. Republished edition by Beacon Press.
[3] Mielach, David. "5 Business Tips from Albert Einstein." *Business News Daily*. April 18, 2012. Boston MA. Retrieved 11.30.19 from www.businessnewsdaily.com/2381-albert-einstein-business-tips.html.

- **RISE POINT** — Concluding summary at the end. This is the main point that I hope you get out of reading that particular chapter.

- **VANTAGE POINT** — Because no man is an island, I have asked people close to me to write from their viewpoint, how living through the shared Atomic Event of Parkinson's with me has impacted their life, hopefully for the better.

This book is designed to do several things:

- Be an instrument of learning for all those who are confronting a Parkinson's diagnoses or any other "Atomic Event" in their life. It also lays out strategies to use in approaching others about the issues that will arise.

- Help others who have just experienced an Atomic Event and are now not quite sure what to do next. This is a "Guidebook" of sorts for recovering from the shock and moving forward.

- Provide a path to follow for those who have decided to thrive in their lives despite the fallout of their Atomic Event. A blueprint to help build the next phase of their life.

- Share a variety of ideas to empower you to set goals for harnessing the energy of your Atomic Event.

One of the strongest forces in nature is the power of human hope. Hope is derived from developing character, perseverance, and joy in the face of overwhelming odds. There is no rational reason for hope. It supersedes the rational thought process. It brings power and the ability of mankind to overcome our present situations. My wish is that if you are reading this book, it brings you hope towards learning to thrive in your life despite the number or intensity of Atomic Events you have or will endure.

After living the first part of my life (pre-Parkinson's) chasing success in the business world and growing my family, Parkinson's has taught me to instead focus my energies on chasing significance in all aspects of my life. I have come to realize that it is a person's legacy, or their ability to positively influence peoples' lives, that is the only truly lasting effect they leave. I live my life by the credo, "Life is an occasion; rise to it!" I pray this book helps to inspire you to do just that.

Even if I should choose to boast, I would not be a fool, because I would be speaking the truth. But I refrain, so no one will think more of me than is warranted by what I do or say, or because of these surpassingly great revelations. Therefore, in order to keep me from becoming conceited, I was given a thorn in my flesh, a messenger of Satan, to torment me. Three times I pleaded with the Lord to take it away from me. But he said to me, "My grace is sufficient for you, for my power is made perfect in weakness." Therefore I will boast all the more gladly about my weaknesses, so that Christ's power may rest on me. That is why, for Christ's sake, I delight in weaknesses, in insults, in hardships, in persecutions, in difficulties. For when I am weak, then I am strong.
2 Corinthians 12:6-10

CHAPTER 1

ATOMIC EVENTS

THE CLASH OF THE "OLD NORMAL"
AND THE "NEW NORMAL"

In February of 2011, my oldest daughter married her long-time Australian boyfriend. They wanted to have a destination wedding, high in the mountain snows of Estes Park, Colorado. Most of the attending Aussies had never seen snow, so this was a perfect opportunity for them to experience it. As the father of the bride, I took charge of renting the limousines to get most of the "Roos" from the chapel to the wedding destination site, because not only were they used to driving on the other side of the road, none of them had ever driven in snow conditions. Double trouble.

I rode to the chapel with my daughter and her bridesmaids. As soon as we got in the limousine, everyone commented on the beautiful fragrance of the wedding bouquets. Then I noticed I couldn't smell anything. Jokingly

I thought maybe if you BUY the flowers you can't smell them. All that expense must have impaired my olfactory system. I didn't know it then, but it was a Parkinson's clue.

When the time for the ceremony began, my daughter and I stood at the back of the church. Between the two of us, a million thoughts were swirling around in our minds as we looked at each other. One thought I couldn't ignore was that I didn't want her to sense my trembling hand while we took that life-changing stroll down the aisle to the front of the church. I wanted this day to be perfect for her.

As we entered the church, I placed her hand on my left arm so she would not feel my tremors — at least from my hand. My knees were shaking as well, but that is to be expected when you give your oldest daughter away.

My fear that something was wrong was not new. I noticed a small tremor in the fingers of my right hand in 2009. While driving, my pinkie finger on my right hand would tremble. I mentioned it to my general practitioner, and he came up with the diagnosis of Benign Essential Tremor. He speculated that this could be nerve damage I sustained while playing sports in my youth. Sounded good to me. At my next yearly check-up, the tremor had moved to my entire right hand. He still thought it was Benign Essential Tremor, with perhaps more nerve damage than we originally thought. It was annoying, but I was okay with that diagnosis.

Jump ahead to 2011 and my fear was becoming more real. After the wedding reception, I asked my wife if she had a shampoo with a distinct smell. She of course did, but when I lathered up, I could not smell anything. After showering, I got online and typed the words, "tremor and no smell". One word popped up; it started with a "P" and ended with "arkinson's". What should have been one of the greatest days of my life — giving my daughter's hand in marriage — turned out to be an, "Oh, crap!" moment when I realized what I might be dealing with.

Over the next couple of months while I waited for an appointment with a neurologist, fear was building up. How bad might this be? The first underground shock waves of the Atomic Event were already beginning. Like a seismometer before an earthquake, I could sense the needle jolting up and down. I had no choice but to ignore it and keep living my life, hoping my shampoo self-diagnosis might be wrong.

My deepest fear played out before my eyes as my symptoms became more noticeable to others. I am faithful about going to yoga class. During the time before my official diagnosis, people in my class pointed out my trembling hand. I stood true to my Benign Essential Tremor diagnosis. I was asked to teach a yoga class to help out an instructor. In the process of moving to the warrior two pose in which your arms are fully extended, shoulder height, away from your body I turned to look at the class. Everyone in the class was shaking their right hand, which mimicked my tremor. That's when I knew my secret was out and my deepest and darkest fears were coming true.

On April 26, 2011, I heard what I had been fearing, "You have Parkinson's Disease." Even though I was convinced before the appointment that I had Parkinson's Disease (PD), it was still an incredible shock to have it professionally confirmed by the neurologist. I was now officially a "Parkie."

Those four words, "You have Parkinson's Disease," started the largest Atomic Event in my life to date. Other Atomic Events have followed since then, like cancer. Before I go on, do you remember my previous description of what I mean by an Atomic Event? They are the events that happen in your life — divorce, cancer, or the loss of a loved one — that change your life as you have known it. The change is forever. I describe it as the collision of unexpected and unwanted events clashing with the daily demands of your normal life, which creates an explosion of unintended negative consequences that permanently change your life view.

The explosion is charged with such force that it changes your worldview for the balance of your existence. You never look at your life in the same way as you once did. This explosion, which you can do nothing about, gives off an energy force so strong that it could completely destroy your

4 RISING ABOVE PARKINSON'S

life. Or, if properly harnessed, can actually enhance your life as it has mine. That is going to be the core lesson from this book.

I have always been a driven person. As I've described myself earlier, I'm a hard-charging, Type A, Warlord of Commerce. I think it stems from always trying to prove myself worthy of my parents' praise and attention. I was the middle child of the family and had a number of medical and hearing problems in my childhood. My hearing problems led to a delay and stunting of my growth, and I weighed only 25 lbs. when I was 5-years-old. By the time I graduated from high school, I was just 5' tall and weighed 105 lbs. My older brother, who is highly intelligent and athletic, was a hard person to follow in school and sports. My sister was the apple of my father's eye — and like many daughters — she commanded his undying devotion. This is no one's fault. It is just human nature that parents seem to connect to one child more than another. Regardless, I was always trying to prove myself.

I did learn quickly in life to play to my strengths, and one strength was the ability to influence people. I have always had a gift of being able to read other people quickly. The combination of my (formerly) small stature and gift of influence allows me to have a positive impact on others. It has led me in a lifelong pursuit of implementing thought models to help people see the direction they should go. I call this positive use of my gift "influence with integrity". Like all gifts, you have to be mindful of how you deploy them in your life. I believe through learning and working with models, you can get people to see the vision of what needs to be accomplished in order to achieve the desired goal.

Over time, I have learned how to harness my positive and negative emotional energy turning them into something worthwhile. That is not to say that I don't have really horrible days, fears and anxiety, but I always come back to the solutions that I describe in this book. Whether you have PD, cancer, or some other debilitating or degenerative disease, I hope and pray that the ideas set forth in this book will help you harness the negative energy which comes with a similar diagnosis. Moreover, I wish you the ability to transform this harnessed energy into hope, joy, grace, and the promise of a better quality of life.

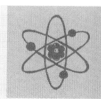

MODEL:
THERAPEUTIC WRITING

I was recently at a Parkinson's support group meeting in which a college professor of Creative Writing led us through an exercise in writing poetry to express our feelings about PD. I had never written any poetry in my life and was fairly skeptical of the process, but I followed along. I wrote the following poem in about seven minutes, never lifting the pen. It just flowed out of me.

In this poem, I tried to convey the effects that having Parkinson's has had in my life. While it shakes me in some of the most essential places of my being (family, health, and work) Parkinson's has actually moved me towards a deeper faith, awareness, and acceptance of my role in the world. I have tried to express how Parkinson's has led me through a distinct progression in my life. At first I felt like I had been "hit by a Mack truck", now I see I'm moving toward enlightenment or the blossoming of my new life potential. I think of my progression as taking the form of a helix[4], slowly rising, as opposed to an unproductive pendulum, just swinging back and forth between good days and bad days.

I hope my poem helps you to understand how I deal with the drudgery of living with Parkinson's every waking moment of every day. If this poem can shed some light on dealing with your Atomic Event in a brighter fashion, then my words have come back to me fulfilled!

---

[4] Helix, noun, he·lix, 'hē-liks. Something spiral in form. *Merriam-Webster*. Retrieved 11.30.19 from www.merriam-webster.com/dictionary/helix.

GOD'S GRACE IS ENOUGH
by Greg Ritscher

I knew it, before I heard it
     Always trust your gut instinct
"You have Parkinson's". Tell me something I don't know
     Parkinson's starts in the same place (gut)
Lewy Bodies building; axioms aflamed; dendrites adrift
     Words you never want to hear
You know, an "Atomic Event"
     The rest of your life blown-up
"Normal" is not normal anymore
     Your life will never be the same
No known cause; no known cure
     Perseverance builds hope, thru character
What will the new normal be?
     God's plan, not mine
Future Expectations Appear Real (F.E.A.R.)
     A loving wife, children, and friends' prayers
I was happy being a Warlord of Commerce
     Did not know I could be loved so much
The thrill of the kill; the taste of blood
     I learned that, "My life is not about me"
Unwanted tremors shake digits
     "Shaken, not stirred" reaches other's hearts
Now thoughts disappear mid-sentence
     Will I be able to live, what I used to preach?
Emotion ignited, tears at the drop of a word
     Diseased Ambassador ... set free
Night Terrors, the Tiger-man is loose
     Oh, the peace that passes all understanding
Fatigue, too tired to sleep
     More "On" than "Off"
Drugs three times a day
     Just masks the pain; why do I even pay?

Quiet voice ... what did you say?
    Kinder, gentler words sing from my mouth
Swallowing, choking, and drool
    God's grace, oh what a powerful force
Gone are hoop teams and tying flies
    The view from the top of a 14'er; priceless!
My life is not falling apart
    It is falling into place
My life is upended
    Just as God had intended for me!

The quality of your life will largely depend on how you learn to handle and redirect the negative energy of your Atomic Events.

RISE POINT:
BECOME AN ASCENDING HELIX

Your Atomic Event might involve Parkinson's or some other catastrophic disruption. Regardless of the initial form this event takes as it bursts into your life, I want you to see it as a twisting helix. You can either let it spiral downward — out of control; or you can choose to rise with it, as it forces you to gain new understanding and discover a renewed sense of purpose in your existence.

VANTAGE POINT:

PHYLIS RITSCHER
WIFE AND BEST FRIEND FOR LIFE

Atomic Event is a good way to describe a Parkinson's Disease diagnosis. Suddenly, time is divided into an uninvited "Before" and "After". Your life as you knew it is gone, and you are part of a club that you never wanted to join. A day or two after his diagnosis, Greg and I talked about how God could use this situation for good. That soon after his diagnosis, he actually said that he could be a spokesperson to help others with PD.

Looking back, it is amazing to me that he could think of others so soon after the diagnosis. I was filled with fear and questions about our unknown future, because Atomic Events do not just affect one person. The ripple effect is wide and those closest are deeply affected. Yet somehow, I also knew deep down that God would indeed use this situation for good, because Greg is always seeking to influence others for good.

Since his diagnosis, I have seen Greg truly thrive. He lives his life with intentionality and focus, always striving to be better and stronger than before. He inspires others simply by the way he lives his life every single day. He chooses not to be defined by a disease but instead to re-define his life for the BETTER because of his disease. Greg has always been a person who prides himself on living by his principles and convictions. Parkinson's Disease has given him the opportunity to put those convictions into action in a deeper and more meaningful way. This doesn't mean that it never gets him down, or that he doesn't have bad days, because he does.

His focus is not on the hard parts of living with this disease but is on the positive impact he can make so he doesn't stay in the low spots for long.

So, as you read this book, you need to know that what he is sharing is the real deal. It is not simply positive thoughts, high ideals, or wishful thinking. Greg is living what he is sharing with the readers of this book. As his wife, I see him getting up while it is still dark outside to work out every day. He prioritizes being part of and building his PD support system: belonging to a support group, boxing with Parkie buddies, attending conferences and events. I have seen him participate in a myriad of research studies as he foresees those in future generations who might benefit from a cure. I hear him talking with hurting people who have recently found out they have Parkinson's. I get messages and emails from friends, and friends of friends who have been diagnosed, because they have heard that Greg might be able to help.

Not every idea or model that Greg shares in these chapters will work for or resonate with everyone. But underneath the ideas and facts, I hope you will see his deep faith and hear his heart to turn something difficult into a message of hope for others who are suffering or facing difficulty. Each of us will face challenges, crises, illnesses, and losses in our lives. Many people face situations that are far more devastating than living with PD. I pray that this book will be an encouragement to many by providing the tools and inspiration to thrive in the midst of whatever life brings. And most of all, that it will give you hope!

For I know the plans I have for you," declares the Lord, "plans to prosper you and not to harm you, plans to give you hope and a future. Then you will call on me and come and pray to me, and I will listen to you.
Jeremiah 29:11-12

CHAPTER 2

THE SHAKING PALSY

PARKINSON'S KNOWLEDGE
FOR THE UNINITIATED

I myself had heard of Parkinson's Disease before I even showed symptoms but I really knew nothing about it. I started my quest for PD knowledge after my diagnosis. I strongly believe that if you can understand the impact of any stimuli on both your mind and body, you can then better control your emotional and behavioral responses. This chapter will give you a basic working foundation you can continue to build on as you learn more about this degenerative disease.

The history of Parkinson's disease begins with Dr. James Parkinson.[5] He wrote a scholarly review in 1817 entitled, "Essay on the Shaking Palsy". It described his observation of six case studies and three patients seen on the streets of London. Jean-Martin Charcot built on this work over

[5] Lewis, Patrick. "James Parkinson: The Man Behind the Shaking Palsy". *Parkinson's Life*.eu. 2019. Retrieved 1.2.20 from https://parkinsonslife.eu/james-parkinson-the-man-behind-the-shaking-palsy/.

fifty years later with much more detailed descriptions of the major motor disorders, especially on bradykinesia (stiffness). There are traditional East Indian texts and ancient Chinese writings which describe various symptoms of Parkinson, but western medicine recognizes Dr. Parkinson as the pioneer researcher of the disease.

What causes Parkinson's disease? A good question; no one really knows. It was first observed in patients when approximately 70% of a person's substantia nigra — a section of the basal ganglia in your brain — died off. The body could no longer produce enough dopaminergic agents to allow the nervous system to operate smoothly. Parkinson's is classified as an idiopathic[6] disease, which means professionals are not sure what causes Parkinson's. To this day, there is no known cure for Parkinson's.

An array of treatments and therapies have been put forward as the number of people living with the disease explodes. There is little chance for science, through empirical studies, to isolate a cure as there are too many variables of how the disease impacts people. The Baby Boomer generation is aging into prime Parkinson's diagnosis age range. The current number of new diagnoses, 60,000 per year, should triple in size over the next ten years. You can do the math on that one!

There are schools of thought that believe one of the causes may come from a genetic predisposition to the disease, as several genes — such as PARK1, PARK4, GBA, and LRRK2 — have been identified as having a significant risk factor associated with them. Obtaining a genetic code report from a reputable lab could be very helpful for you to have, and this would also assist researchers of Parkinson's disease. By sharing this information with appropriate entities, we can only help to reduce, even eliminate our lack of knowledge regarding what causes Parkinson's.

Unfortunately, I know many people who do not want to do the genetic testing for fear of what they might learn. In the next chapter we are going to go in depth on the subject of fear, but for now I want you to consider that if we can overcome fear, we can gain much more clarity. You can then

---

[6] Idiopathic, adjective, id·i·o·path·ic, i-dē-a-ˈpa-thik. Arising spontaneously or from an obscure or unknown cause. *Merriam-Webster*. Retrieved 2.5.20 from www.merriam-webster.com/dictionary/idopathic.

discover why learning about the disease can be an important journey in staying as healthy as you can be. When you are first diagnosed and hit with the reality of your mortality, fear is a natural phenomenon. Your mind is attempting to wrap around this new normal for you, which is only partially known. The quicker you can intellectually learn the truth about ALL facets of your Parkinson's disease, the quicker you can dissipate the fear from your mindset.

Ingestion of environmental toxins — from ground water or foods — has been another long-thought cause. This factor is harder to study because it is probably a long-term impact from whatever toxins you were exposed to many years ago. Those toxins now reside within your gut, and they will eventually lead to the death of the dopamine producing brain cells.

Intracellular damage from a build-up of alpha-synuclein proteins, called Lewy bodies, is another suspected culprit. For some reason, people with Parkinson's have a propensity to have their alpha-synuclein start coiling into structures, which then begin clotting together to form damaging bodies within the cell. Eventually, enough of these alpha-synuclein structures clot together and form Lewy bodies. It is believed this tying together of intracellular "trash" is what kills the cells. Once you lose +70% of these brain cells in the substantia negra, you start to exhibit signs of Parkinson's.

Whether it's the brain, genetics, gut, or toxins, Parkinson's has no known bio-markers to scan for. Still to this day, it is diagnosed through subjective clinical observation by neurologists. Pharmacological agents merely mask the symptoms, and neurosurgical treatments appear to have a short life span of effectiveness. Hence, our best hope may be in the form of an accidental cure, similar to the discovery of penicillin. "One sometimes finds what one is not looking for" is a quote attributed to Sir Alexander Fleming.[7] He was the Scottish researcher credited with the almost accidental discovery of antibiotics in 1928, ironically after being away from the lab for two weeks on vacation. In time, it is likely that research will find multiple biomarkers, which may lead to better understanding.

---

[7] "Alexander Fleming". *Science History.* Updated December 5, 2017. Retrieved 12.7.19 from https://www.sciencehistory.org/historical-profile/alexander-fleming.

Everyone's Parkinson's expresses itself with a different combination of motor, non-motor, and psychological effects. Some people tremor, while others exhibit bradykinesia (stiffness of muscles), and still others show signs of dyskinesia (jerking spasms of muscles). This contributes to a fair amount of misdiagnosis by general practitioners.

How Common Is Parkinson's?

The lead-in heading to an article in the Journal of Parkinson's Disease, "The Emerging Evidence of the Parkinson's Pandemic,"[8] clearly defined Parkinson's as a pandemic. A pandemic is a disease or malady that extends over a large geographical area and tends to migrate due to changing life factors (ultra-processed foods, increased toxic chemical intake via alcohol and drugs, ever limited physical activity, etc.), which experiences exponential growth.

Parkinson's Disease is all this and more. It has grown by 118% to 6.2 million people worldwide from 1990 to 2015. Though it is non-infectious (you cannot "catch" Parkinson's from someone who has it), no one is immune to the disease. Largely driven by an aging population with increased exposure to the harmful effects of industrialization, Parkinson's is shifting in scope from a Western to an Eastern hemisphere dominating disease. China and Japan are especially fertile ground for this pandemic because of their rapidly aging societies and large populations. The number of people worldwide with Parkinson's is projected to exceed 12 million by 2040. That is a lot of Parkies!

Once you know what to look for — dead arm hanging from a shoulder; slow, shuffling feet; and a far-away, disinterested look on their face — "Parkies" are fairly easy to spot in a crowd.

Suffice it to say that no one knows your body better than you. If you sense something is amiss, please take the time to visit a trained medical professional to get a proper diagnosis. Be aware that no two people's

---

[8] Dorsey, E. Ray, Sherer, Todd, Okun, Michael S., Bloem, Bastiaan R. "The Times They Are a-Changin': Parkinson's Disease 20 Years from Now". Vol. 8, No. 1, pp. S3-S8, 2018. *Journal of Parkinson's Disease*. Retrieved 11.30.19 from content.iospress.com/articles/journal-of-parkinsons-disease/jpd181474#d.

Parkinson's Disease have the same group of symptoms. I tremor on the right side of my body but have few major twitches (called dyskinesias). I cannot smell anything, but others still have both their sense of smell and taste. My point is that just because your symptoms don't look like mine, does not mean you don't have Parkinson's or some other neurological disorder. Early diagnosis means earlier interventions.

How Do I Talk to Others About Parkinson's
By now you might have come to terms with the fact that you, or maybe someone that you care about, has Parkinson's Disease. But you might be asking yourself some of the following questions:

- HOW do I tell others about my diagnosis?
- WHAT ramifications will follow once I start telling people that I have Parkinson's?
- WHEN do I tell them that Parkinson's has entered my life?
- WHERE is my life with Parkinson's going to take me?
- WHO all should I tell, and in what order?

For me this was fairly straight forward. I am a very open person and believe that you can never get or give enough information to help you jump over the hurdles of life. My wife was with me when I got the official diagnosis, so she already knew. Right away, I called each of my children, siblings, and parents to let them know. Once told, my friends, mentors, and Bible study pals began praying for me.

I decided to update my will and check in with my financial advisor to "Get my house in order". My employer had already observed that I probably had Parkinson's, so I confided in him. Then, I decided which business vendors and customers I wanted to personally tell. Today's technology took over, and within a short time I was getting calls from a variety of business associates asking about my disease and what it meant for me.

Everyone's situation is unique (just like your Parkinson's symptoms). I have mentored several middle-aged business leaders who were recently diagnosed with Parkinson's in how to go about telling various people in their lives that they have the disease and just exactly what it means. Many middle-aged men do not want to show any cracks in their armor, especially in the business world. I myself was fifty-five-years-old when diagnosed, and still very active in the business world. Parkinson's Disease that exhibits certain motor skill symptoms (i.e. tremors) will be very hard to disguise in a stress-filled work environment. If this type of scenario worries you, I'd say preparation is the key.

Parkinson's psychological impacts on your personality and demeanor are easily noticed by others. It would be virtually impossible to hide or not explain these symptoms with someone who knows you very well. This will also give the people who care for you most the ability to express their love through their service to you. My daughters taught me that. My advice is to just tell it like it is. This strategy of honesty will show you who your real friends are!

Most people have heard of Parkinson's, but they have no idea of what it physically does to your body. Few have any awareness of the problematic non-motor symptoms. My suggestion is to sit down and write out a complete list of people you want to tell personally, then prioritize the list. Be prepared to describe briefly what Parkinson's is: an idiopathic disease caused by the brain's inability to produce enough dopamine for your nervous system to operate properly.

Discuss that, at present, there is no known cause and no known cure. Be sure to provide your people with quality, valid sources of information to follow up with. If you are a social-media type of person, be sure to send out correct information the first time to avoid mis-interpretations.

MODEL:
MAKE TEN FROM NINE MARKS

Take a look at the figure below. By mentally rearranging the elements, see if you can make this figure represent TEN. Oh, by the way, you cannot add a single mark to the figure. Give yourself 30 seconds. Ready, go!

Parkinson's is a lot like this model. How do you rearrange the parts of your life to increase its quality, when you cannot add anything to your life? You are forced to look at it differently. This model just represents the number nine, it is not inherently "nine." Your mind directed you to that conclusion by associating the figure with the value of nine.

As soon as I mentioned NOT being able to add anything to the exercise, mental limitations set in. This is akin to being told about all the negative effects that Parkinson's will bring to your everyday life. It appears to be an impossible task. (See *Endnotes F.* page 190 for the correct answer.)

If you switch your perspective from merely seeing a quantity of 9, to visually constructing the word TEN, you will quickly find that TEN is composed of nine straight lines. Similarly, after your diagnosis, your paradigm about what a "normal life" can change. Your attitude and your life expectations could be realigned to fit a whole new view of the future.

All my life, I have taken pride in myself on being an excellent decision maker. I saw emotion as a weakness and a limitation in making good decisions. One of the many symptoms of Parkinson's is that it makes you a much more emotional thinker. Now, I often cry when watching children's movies with my grandchildren. If I were still at the "Nine" marks thinking level, I would see this as a problem. After hearing from so many people that they enjoy my decisions and actions more now that I incorporate emotion into my interactions with them, I have come to see emotion as moving me to a "TEN" marks level of thought and communication.

Don't get me wrong; I am not belittling the symptoms of Parkinson's Disease and its effects on your mind and body. Believe me, I live with them every day. What I am trying to convey is that we have the power of Response-Ability in our lives for any Atomic Event that side-swipes our path.

The biblical story of Job comes to mind. I'll recount a shortened version: Job was an extremely wise, wealthy, and God-fearing man. God even brags about him to the devil who has been wandering the earth causing trouble. The devil responds by saying Job is this way because God protects him from all evil. A bet is put in place between God and the devil — the devil says that Job will curse God just as soon as the devil is done piling terrible things onto his life.

Immediately, the devil kills all ten of Job's children, destroys all of his crops and cattle, and decimates all of Job's home and possessions! Talk about an Atomic Event! Yet, Job still will not curse God for these terrible calamities in his life. The devil then brings in three of Job's friends to dissuade him from not blaming God for the terrible mess, but Job stays true to his faith. Eventually, God drives away the devil then restores to Job more than double everything he lost.[9]

So, whether it is the patience of Job or my learning to add some emotion to my decision making and communication, I have in fact become a better communicator. Apparently, by learning to look at all the different aspects of your life from a broader view, you will only improve your overall effectiveness.

---

[9] *Job.* 42:12-15

If we learn to look at all of the perspectives of the situation we are faced with, we can figure out a way to rise with our challenges. Just as Job did not blame God for the terrible things that happened to him, I have come to see that I must learn to live with the effects of Parkinson's in my life, becoming an even better person because of them. In an odd way, Parkinson's has made me a more significant person through my ability to positively impact other people's lives.

RISE POINT:
REMAIN POSITIVE

Atomic Events happen in everyone's life. You are not being picked on! Learn a number of model approaches in the rest of this book to deal with the adversity you face. Now that you have some working knowledge of Parkinson's, it's up to you to choose whether you are going to take a path that gradually falls over time, or one that gradually rises as life pushes at you from various directions.

VANTAGE POINT:

MEREDITH ROBERT,
MD, PT, DPT

Parkinson's Disease – Then to Now

There was a time, not that long ago, when we thought of Parkinson's as one disease. This disease had several key symptoms that could be managed with medications. The typical image that would surface in medical textbooks and later on internet searches, included an old, frail man hunched over with a cane. He had little lines around his feet and hands to indicate a shuffling motion with his feet and a shaking of his hands.

Parkinson's today is viewed as a spectrum disorder — or umbrella term — for a much larger syndrome that can take many forms. We still find typical Parkinson's in the center of this spectrum with its classic symptoms of slowness, stiffness, tremor, and balance problems — aka bradykinesia, rigidity, and postural instability.

However, we also find under this umbrella atypical, or Parkinson's Plus syndromes, and secondary Parkinson's. These categories of Parkinson's offer different symptom profiles and presentations, while still retaining some of the same characteristics of typical Parkinson's. They can be harder to diagnose, treat, relate to, or understand. There is so much we still don't know and are learning about the umbrella of Parkinson's. One thing we do know is that no two people are or will look alike despite what "type" of Parkinson's they may be diagnosed with. Most importantly, despite what your Parkinson's looks like, you still have the control and ability to do things each day to fight back against the disease.

Parkinson's – The Cafeteria Disease

Many of us start the Parkinson's journey by trying to make sense of what has been given to us, and what exactly Parkinson's is. With today's modern technology and the gift of the internet with engine search features, instinctively we go there first, only to find information overload. We find a laundry list of symptoms that appears never-ending. It is normal to become overwhelmed and even a little afraid of all we see, thinking, "Is this what is going to happen to me?"

How I prefer to make sense of Parkinson's is to think of it like your old school cafeteria. Each of us walks through the line with our tray, getting a scoop of this, a scoop of that, avoiding this and avoiding that. We all walk through the same cafeteria to fill our tray with choices we made from the same smorgasbord. However, when we sit down and compare our trays, they all look different. Parkinson's is just the cafeteria we all walk through; yet, each of us walks out with a different tray of symptoms. Just because something may be a symptom of Parkinson's, does not mean it will be a symptom that you experience on your tray. This is helpful to keep in mind as you learn more about the disease itself. Just because someone else has a certain set of symptoms, it does not mean you will have those, too. No two people with Parkinson's are alike.

Developing Resilience

Resilience, grit, hardiness ... despite what you choose to call it, resilience is the most essential ingredient to the first key decision you are faced with when you hear those four words, "You have Parkinson's Disease". Who gets to be in control, Parkinson's or you? Parkinson's is the dark, scary alleyway riddled with real threats, challenges, and moments where defeat may occur. Nevertheless, only you can choose how to enter that alley. You can enter it with your bodyguards, guns blazing, plan of attack in hand, ready to change strategies when needed, then you can ask for help when things don't go as planned. Or you could enter alone, lay down, succumb, and let the challenges of the dark alley have its way with you. Either way, you get to choose. What can guide this choice — make it more instinctual — are our past experiences and how they have helped us to develop resilience.

First Steps Forward

Our lives provide us with challenges large and small. Through those challenges, we test our resilience. We learn that when we want something, there are things we can do large and small to help us get it. Sometimes, this is formal such as acquiring a particular job or promotion. To achieve this, we study hard in school, get a mentor, give ourselves experiences that help us slowly move towards this goal. At other times, these challenges are less intentional and goal-directed such as when we find ourselves doing our best to survive being a new parent. We ask friends and family for advice, get help in unique ways, read parenting books on how to improve our infant's sleep, or find joy in the little things instead of thinking of them as burdensome tasks.

Whether intentional and highly structured, or unintentional and fly-by-the-seat-of-our-pants, we learn we always have a say. Each moment, each situation, we get a choice to step forward with specific actions. We build our confidence through success over these challenges and meeting these goals. This confidence stays with us and boosts us up when challenging situations demand us to be resilient. So, when life throws us it's biggest challenge yet, we can get back up, dust ourselves off, and take the next step forward.

Discovering What is Possible

Despite the daunting feeling that comes with the word "Parkinson's", you can live a meaningful, fulfilled life that is abundant with happiness and purpose. You may have Parkinson's, but Parkinson's does not have you! There are real things you can do to fight back against the disease. The key is you need to believe it is possible. In medical research, patients who enjoy a high quality of life are the ones who believe they can fight back despite what they have been diagnosed with. They have a high level of resilience, or in the medical world we call this self-efficacy. Then, they use this resilience along with the power of their community to optimize what they have the most control over.

With Parkinson's Disease, we have found those who have been diagnosed do best when they use exercise as medicine, manage stress, eat healthy, and work with a team to optimize their medications and manage symptoms. These are all things that you have the control to act on. What is most important here is not what type of exercise you do or exactly what your diet is made up of, but that you believe you are in control of your disease, not that the disease is in control of you. When you are in control, you actively make an effort to put things into place — a plan of action — to prevent potential problems and improve current ones.

However, we recognize that we are all human and changing our health behaviors is, well, hard! Now, if only I could put exercise in a pill …. So, to help us be more successful in overcoming barriers and truly changing our health behavior habits, we need to call on our community to help us. Community can be many different things to different people. Often, we need a variety of different communities to support us. Our family members, close friends, co-workers, neighbors, our exercise class, a spiritual group, or a support group are just a few examples. These communities help to encourage us, boost us when our spirits are low, give us ideas when we face barriers, and hold us accountable to do what we say we are going to do. They help us along the way and support us through this journey. Because, well, "It takes a village …."

Your Challenge – Yes, Homework!
1. Identify what your Parkinson's symptoms tray looks like. What are two or three challenges Parkinson's is giving you currently? I.e.: It is difficult to sleep more than 4-6 hours a night.
   - What would you like to experience instead? I.e.: I would like to wake up feeling rested after a full night's sleep.
   - What is one action you could take this week to help you start moving towards this new reality?
     > I will start putting good sleep habits into my schedule by going to bed at the same time each night and waking up at the same time each morning.
     > Or, I will reduce my screen time prior to bed.

- How can you tap into your existing network to find support for setting and achieving a plan towards waging a war with Parkinson's? If you had to go into battle, who would you put on your team to help you win, and what strengths do they bring? Some may be good listeners, some good problem solvers, and others might hold you accountable to your word. List three people or groups and how they can help you.

- My spouse will hold me accountable to turn off my computer by 8:00 pm each night so I can get into bed and be asleep by 10:00 pm.
- My neighbor will meet with me each morning at 8:00 am for a walk around the park.
- I will find a local support group to help me learn how others have coped with this situation.

2. What are your personal strengths? What have you done well in your lifetime that you could use here to help you fight back against Parkinson's? I.e. Maybe you are a good researcher, a good networker, or very organized. These skills could help you to:

- Gather information to prepare a plan.
- Help you find the right people to put on your team.
- Be organized so you can optimize time with your doctor at the next appointment.

The Lord blessed the latter part of Job's life more than the former part.
Job 42:12a

CHAPTER 3

FACING YOUR F.E.A.R.

FUTURE EXPECTATIONS APPEAR REAL

It's bad enough to hear, "You have Parkinson's Disease." But the worst part is all the fearful thoughts which race through your mind: "Will I become disabled?" "What will I do about work?" "How long until I can't drive a car anymore?" "Can I maintain my independence?" "How will Parkinson's interfere with my dreams and plans for my family?" "Will I see my grandchildren graduate, get married, or have children?"

All my life, I have been a planner. I'm orderly and I'm a very detail-oriented individual. Suddenly, my life's plan was going up in smoke and I wanted to know, "Why?"

F.E.A.R. can change your bucket list from climbing a 14,000' mountain to just getting out of bed in the morning!

Even before I left the doctor's office, I wanted to know as much as I could about what I would be facing. Thoughts of, "Why me?" "How did I get this disease?" were on my mind. In my ignorance, I thought there was a cure. I thought if I knew everything ahead of time, the fear might go away or at least slow down.

As the evidence mounted that PD was a permanent part of my life, I tried to rationalize where it came from. "How did I get this?" "Was it genetic, an environmental toxin, or just some terrible spell of bad luck?" I didn't know of anyone in my family who had Parkinson's Disease. However, once I learned the symptoms and traits of PD, I'm relatively sure my maternal grandmother had this disease, but she was never properly diagnosed.

I asked the doctors for all the information they could give me on how I got this and how I was going to fight it. My first response was to use knowledge to fight my fear. I thought if I could read everything about Parkinson's, I would notice something everyone else had overlooked.

Fear, in all its various forms — anger, failure, hopelessness, hostility, passive aggressiveness — is a common denominator in human behavior. While everyone's Parkinson's symptoms are different, fear of negative outcomes pervades all of us. Fear is your mind assessing the current situation and believing some form of trouble or loss is imminent.

Fear is a deep-rooted emotion, originally designed to keep us alive via the fight or flight instinct. It's not likely that any of us will be hunted down by a real tiger any time soon. Our "tiger" is our Parkinson's Disease. If we could, we would run the other direction, or else chase it to make it go away. The problem is that it won't go away. No matter how much we try, it is always with us, which creates a perpetual state of anxiety that can eat away at who we are, who we love, and how we want to live our lives.

Victor Frankl, the famous Austrian psychologist I mentioned previously — who survived the Auschwitz POW camp — noticed that human beings have a very unique psychological trait in the animal kingdom: we have

Response-Ability. Animals, when faced with deadly stimuli, resort to either their Fight or Flight response. Either they run from the stimuli (flight) or they turn and attack (fight) it. Humans have the capacity to see a gap between stimulus and response; it is in fact the last ultimate freedom we possess.

We have the power to respond to the Atomic Events in our lives in any way we choose. In this book, I will present several models that will help you learn to thrive despite your Atomic Event.

Ruled by Fear

Incurable diseases can have the same mental impact on us as terrorists and dictators. For example, ISIS uses frequent but geographically limited extreme acts of violence to create an ongoing sense of fear on a global scale. Genghis Khan, Adolf Hitler, and other tyrants pioneered this powerful fear tactic in past centuries. They maintained cultures in which any one individual in a group might be tortured and killed, which instilled a perpetual state of fearful submission in the entire group.

Fear can grow exponentially as your mind continues to expand the depth and breadth of the original threat, and eventually it becomes unrealistic and leads you to take unreasonable actions. From my first day of diagnosis until now, these many years later, I could not have anticipated where I would be today. My fear told me I would be in a wheelchair within a few years, but nine years later my current reality is far from it.

To help me overcome the tendency of deceptive fear, I often use the acronym F.E.A.R. which stands for Future Expectations Appear Real. Fear has to do with loss whether actual or perceived. Fear is derived from the self-talk of your brain playing out a future scenario in which the negative effects far outweigh any possible positive impact.

My fear in discovering I had Parkinson's was twofold. One, I would become a burden to my wife, family, and friends. Two, Parkinson's may have been caused by some genetic malfunction that my children and grandchildren would inherit. Of these two, the latter still concerns me the most. Did I pass down some genetic mutation that would affect my children and their children's future?

This fear is not in my hands. My faith tells me that God is in charge. No matter how much I wish it to be different, God has a plan for me. Philippians 4:13 encourages me that I can do all things — including enduring the effects of a major disease — through Him who strengthens me. His strength is made perfect in my weakness.

The key is to take an 'intrinsic control perspective' of the disease, meaning you need to now see Parkinson's as an inherent part of you. It resides in your body and will influence every part of your life. Parkinson's may delineate what is now possible, drawing imaginary lines around our lives that define very distinct boundaries. However, we cannot let it define who we are, we can choose to limit these boundaries now and in the future. We have the power to cross these boundaries or push them further down the road then we might have originally believed was possible.

This book is designed to show you examples of how I erase those boundaries, or at the very least, I push them out in the future for a later day. I am under no illusion; someday those boundaries will meet me head on. For now, I will continue to push them away.

Creative Destruction

There is a principle attributed to the economist Joseph Schumpeter termed Creative Destruction.[10] In short, some new force brings about the demise of a pre-existing condition, thus positioning the new force to be in place of the old condition.

Ocean waves are a natural example of creative destruction. On your first day at the beach, the waves have created a particular shape and look to the shore line. By the time you see the next wave hit the beach, the shoreline has a brand new look and shape. It is always changing, gradually over time.

---

[10] Cabellero, Ricardo J. "Creative Destruction." *Economics MIT*. Retrieved 11.30.19 from economics.mit.edu/files/1785.

Creative Destruction found in nature has a built-in recovery system. A wave has thousands of gallons of water in it, but the infiltration rate of the sand and the topography of the beach cause the water to drain away before the next wave arrives. Each wave reshapes the beach. Thus, the beach has a system to harness this incredible energy of creative change.

The only things that can change the steady pace and size of the waves are violent storms and earthquakes. Each and every hurricane and tsunami is an Atomic Event to the affected beach. The sheer size and intensity of the waves' tidal surge overruns the drainage capacity of the existing beach. When this happens, a new system of creative destruction forms on the freshly composed beach. The natural process of beach formation cannot be stopped. I recently witnessed this phenomenon in Florida as tropical storm Nestor changed the entire shape and width of Miramar Beach overnight.

Such is the case of Parkinson's. Ever since the day of my diagnosis, I have learned to live within the power and the force of this creative destruction going on in my life. It is my job to harness that energy. No matter how powerfully ugly it is, it is always with me and there is nothing I can do to stop it.

MODEL:
INTERNAL SENSE OF CONTROL

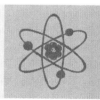

They say "time heals all wounds", but what they do not talk about is how much character it requires to remain perseverant during the time of healing. This vital character and perseverance are ultimately what builds "Response-Ability".

This is called having an "Internal Sense of Control". My Response-Ability starts with the fact that I believe I can choose how to respond to any stimulus that the world throws at me because of the following reasons:

1. Faith teaches me that I know the end-story of my life. As a Christian, I know that Heaven awaits me, and in Heaven we will all have perfect bodies that can harbor no disease. My life with Parkinson's on earth is not my true home, Heaven is. There is a lyric in a song that says, "My life is not falling apart; it's falling into place."[11] This is exactly how I choose to look at having Parkinson's. I am here on earth to be an ambassador to the public for this terrible disease. In all humility, I believe Parkinson's has not yet met a person like me who is better equipped to learn to rise with it in their life.

2. Intellect tells me that I need to learn everything I can about Parkinson's so that I can make wise choices in my "Parkinson's Battle Plan". By intellectually understanding what Parkinson's is and how it affects various aspects of my life, I am in a better position to understand and overcome many of the psychological and non-motor symptoms associated with it. I have to be careful in talking to other people with Parkinson's because not everyone is as motivated as I am to learn all the scientific aspects of the disease.

3. My body needs to experience and learn to deal with the motor symptoms of Parkinson's. I need to learn what a tremor in my face, a frozen muscle in my leg, or dyskinesia in my shoulder feels like when coming on. No one knows your body better than you. More importantly, you need the positive reinforcement that comes with appropriately dealing with these issues, especially when in public. Keeping a light-hearted approach to dealing daily with these issues is great medicine.

4. The final piece of the puzzle is the great elixir: The best drugs I take are the free ones my body produces after a hard workout. Endorphins, peptides, dopamine, and serotonin are all-natural substances released by various parts of your body that give you a great sense of wellbeing and lift your spirits. They are the perfect antidote to Parkinson's nasty batch of neurological distresses. Plus, unlike the prescription drugs commonly prescribed to treat Parkinson's, this set of drugs has no

---

[11] Casting Crowns, "Just Be Held". *Thrive*. 2014. Beach Street and Reunion Records. Retrieved 1.22.2020 from https://castingcrowns.com/music/just-be-held/.

bad side effects. Think about it: our bodies were designed by God to work hard and provide for us. Only in the last three hundred years has society shifted away from being hunters, gatherers, and farmers in a physically-demanding, agronomy-based society. Now, we are an information-based service society that has most of us sitting all day at a desk or computer, which probably makes us less able to combat the effects of diseases such as Parkinson's.

RISE POINT:
RESPONSE-ABILITY

Atomic Events will happen in everyone's life at some point. It is up to us to use these unique opportunities and take Response-Ability — to harness the energy of each event — and develop a game plan to help ourselves and those we love, so we can all overcome F.E.A.R.

VANTAGE POINT:

LINDO PEDRAZA,
SON-IN-LAW

Greg Ritscher is my father-in-law and I have known him since 2007. I am married to Candace, Greg's youngest daughter. Candace and I have been friends since 2006 and got married in 2010. I remember while we were still just friends attending the University of Colorado at Boulder together, she invited me to her parent's house so she could pick up a few things for her dorm room. I remember Greg answering the door shirtless, crossing his arms to keep an eye on me while Candace ran inside to grab her things. I knew in that moment — and every moment since then — that Greg is a strong man.

Greg embodies what I consider to be real strength. I'm sure at this point you're picturing a bodybuilder. He is, but his power comes from something much deeper. Greg has helped me understand what it means to be strong in many different ways.

First, is physical strength. Pretty soon after Candace and I started dating, Greg invited me to play what he called "friendly" basketball with him and his friends on a Saturday morning. Friendly is definitely not the word I would use to describe the level of basketball that was being played. All of the men in that gym were serious athletes and Greg was easily one of the best there. It didn't take long for me to realize just how athletic Greg was as he posted me up, backed me down, and made an easy layup.

After Candace and I got married, Greg invited me to work out with him and I got to witness again first hand just how fit Greg is. We did an hour long crossfit workout, then lifted weights. Additionally, we played a little game I like to call "Anything you can do, I can do better". It was really just a way for him to show me how much stronger he was with every exercise we did. I was blown away by his endurance and strength as he bested me in both categories despite being 30 years my senior.

Second, is mental strength. Greg is easily one of the smartest people I know. I have never met anyone who knows the Bible as well as he does. When Candace and I were dating, I learned Greg writes Bible verses on business cards that he keeps in his car so he can memorize Scripture. I also remember on several occasions during our marriage, Candace gave Greg a call to ask him questions about the Bible. I admire this tremendously and hope to someday be an equal Bible resource for my children.

He also knows more information about wildlife and nature than anyone I have ever met. I remember one time while we were all together on a family vacation, we went to Yellowstone National Park. I got to see how knowledgeable he was about animals and habitat. He told us everything we could ever want to know about Yellowstone's unique ecosystem. I know I can always go to Greg if I have questions about the Bible, business, nature, relationships, or whatever!

Third, is emotional strength. Back on that first day we met, I'll admit I was pretty intimidated by Greg's strength and presence. In getting to know him more, I have come to learn that he isn't afraid to show his softer side. I know how much he loves his wife and daughters because he says it regularly. More importantly, he expresses it by showing up and serving them all the time. Being an attentive and intentional husband and father of three daughters takes lots of emotional intelligence and patience, which I have seen him exhibit regularly. I know modern culture is always telling men that being strong means never showing your emotions, but I believe this is actually one of the biggest myths men face today.

Our culture has this idea that emotional coldness and anger are positive male qualities, while showing empathy and sharing emotions are negative male qualities. This false ideology is one of the reasons I believe so many men commit violent acts on a regular basis. Greg has modeled for me that there are times to expose your emotions and it is okay to share them with your loved ones.

I truly believe that it takes real strength to care for and be vulnerable with your loved ones. Ecclesiastes 3:1, 4 says, *There is a time for everything, and a season for every activity under the heavens .... A time to weep, and a time to laugh; a time to mourn, and a time to dance.* God has given us our emotions and there are appropriate places, times, and ways to express them. Greg has helped remind me of this truth.

Fourth, in my opinion, the most important type of strength is spiritual. I know Greg wakes up early every morning to read his Bible and pray. I have always admired his unwavering faith in God and his willingness to serve others. It is evident that his love of God and desire to do what God wants him to do has strengthened with PD. While being diagnosed with a disease like Parkinson's may have made some people question their faith or doubt God and His plan, Greg has shown tremendous faith.

I have had the privilege of getting to see Greg speak at church several times. Every time he does, he talks about using the experiences in one's life to point people to Christ. 2 Corinthians 5:7 says, *For we live by faith, not by sight*. No one knows what their future holds and no one knows when their life will end. These huge life uncertainties can be scary for some people to think about. This Bible verse tells us to not worry about uncertainty. Rather, we should live our lives with faith in God, and have faith that God's plan for our lives is better than our own plan. Greg lives out that verse everyday. I know Greg didn't have Parkinson's Disease in his life plan, but I can tell you he has chosen to accept God's plan for his life and to use this disease to point people to Christ.

Greg asked me to write about ways in which I have witnessed him change since being diagnosed with Parkinson's Disease. While I am sure you could argue that the disease has made him more in touch with his emotions and more aware that life could end at any point, to me Greg has largely remained the same man of God who loves his family and others. That to me is the most admirable thing about him.

Greg loves God and loves people which is what God, the Maker of the universe, asks us to do everyday. Greg has been a role model to me in so many ways, none more important than being a man of God. I will continue to strive to love God and people like Greg does now, and has done for as long as I have known him. He fulfills Jesus Christ's teaching in Matthew 22:36-40, *"Teacher, which is the greatest commandment in the Law?" Jesus replied: "'Love the Lord your God with all your heart and with all your soul and with all your mind.' This is the first and greatest commandment. And the second is like it: 'Love your neighbor as yourself.' All the Law and the Prophets hang on these two commandments".*

If there is one thing I hope you take away from this book, it is that God exists and He sent His son Jesus Christ to earth to die for our sins so that we can spend eternity with Him in heaven. Greg lives his life for God. I hope the way he lives his life inspires you to live your life for God as much as he has inspired me to do so.

But be sure to fear the Lord and serve him faithfully with all your heart; consider what great things he has done for you.
1 Samuel 12:24

CHAPTER 4

SHAKEN TO THE C.O.O.R.E

CONTROL, ORIGIN, OWNERSHIP, REACH, ENDURANCE

"Oh my God, I'm going to become a burden to my family!" and, "I would rather be dead than be a financial or physical burden to my family." Those were my first thoughts after I heard the neurologist's diagnosis. If I have a disease with no known cause, how am I going to be alive for the discovery of a cure? I had heard of Parkinson's disease, but I never imagined that a healthy, athletic person such as myself could get it. Next came, "So what does this mean for the balance of my life, and is it fatal?" I needed answers, and I needed them quickly.

The neurologist who diagnosed me is known for his passion for research and I immediately enrolled in his current study. As I would come to understand, companies that sponsor research studies prefer to use newly diagnosed patients in drug studies because they do not have a history with any previous medication targeting the new disease in their bodies.

Becoming a Guinea Pig

Now there is nothing wrong with being a guinea pig. In fact, every Parkinson's patient who wants to participate in research should do so until we find a cause and a cure. However, medical professionals need to remember that a person who has just heard that they have an idiopathic disease, that they did nothing to deserve, may not be ready to be in a study. Greater sensitivity to newly diagnosed people should be exercised.

I have spoken several times to the incoming class of medical students at the University of Colorado Medical Health Center in Denver. Each time I like to leave them with one final thought which I believe will help them become better doctors. That is, "No one cares how much you know until they know how much you care."[12] Anyone dealing with an individual who is experiencing an Atomic Event in their lives should take those words to heart.

Compounding Atomic Events

It was December of 2015 and the Christmas season was in full swing. Watching my grandsons participate in family holiday traditions made my life more joyful and complete. I was enrolled in a Parkinson's study that required monthly blood analysis. I got a call from the lab saying that my PSA level had shot up to 6.9 in less than two months. I went to see a specialist at the Urology Center of Colorado. After getting some lab tests, I learned that I had advanced prostate cancer.

"Oh great, another Atomic Event for me to deal with and this one is far more lethal!"

My thoughts ran the gambit from "Why me?" to "Here we go again." It seemed like life was piling it on! I was shaken to the core. Up to this point, I saw myself as a healthy, vibrant individual. I now no longer "just" had a life-altering disease; I also had a life-threatening disease. It was the Christmas season and I didn't want to alarm my friends and family with yet another health concern in my life. Instead of being a time of celebration,

---

[12] Roosevelt, Theodore. "The Man in the Arena". 4.23.1910.The Roosevelt Center at Dickinson State University. Retrieved 3.28.20 from https://www.theodorerooseveltcenter.org/Learn-About-TR/TR-Quotes?page=3

it was a season of new fears and concerns. Being a transparent person, I knew I needed to share this diagnosis with my family, pronto! But I wanted to access medical information and resources first, so that I could alleviate their fears (and mine) as much as possible.

My faith and my Type A personality quickly took over. I consulted physicians and learned as much as I could about the various treatment options available. I decided on a course of treatment, which would include 45 days of modulated radiation. It was the hardest thing I have ever had to physically endure in my life. There was a silver lining. As part of participating in a Parkinson's study and getting monthly lab results, we caught the cancer early, the treatments worked, and I have been cancer free ever since.

MODEL:
ADVERSITY QUOTIENT

"Chance favors the prepared mind",[13] so I quickly turned to a model I learned in the book *Adversity Quotient*,[14] by Dr. Paul Stoltz. Dr Stoltz refers to a concept called C.O.O.R.E., which helps a person understand and embrace the adversity in their lives, enabling them to chart the course for the positive outcomes we all seek. C.O.O.R.E. is an acronym that stands for:

Control – To what degree did you have Control over the cause of the adversity in your life? Parkinson's Disease strikes people randomly, while something like lung cancer has a huge correlation with smoking. Often, it is worse to think you did nothing wrong; you just got the short end of the stick.

[13] Pasteur, Louis. Forbes Quotes Thoughts on the Business of Life. *Forbs*. Retrieved 3.14.2020 from https://www.forbes.com/quotes/6145/
[14] Stoltz, Dr. Paul G. *Adversity Quotient: Turning Obstacles into Success*, 1999, Wiley. Hoboken NJ.

Origin – What is the Origin of the adversity in your life? Parkinson's has no known cause, so it may lead you to feel picked on or unlucky in life. It is not like you ate the wrong foods or are paying the price of a previous addiction.

Ownership – To what degree are you going to take Ownership of dealing with the effects of the Atomic Event in your life? Your daily attitude is one of the very few things you actually can control.

Reach – To what degree will this adversity Reach into your life? Parkinson's, with its motor, non-motor, and psychological symptoms, impacts your life as a constant, overarching presence.

Endurance – How long will you have to Endure this adversity, which has a negative impact on your life? With no known cause, and worse yet, no known cure, Parkinson's will disaffect you for the balance of your life.

Applying the C.O.O.R.E Adversity Quotient Model
In *The Adversity Quotient*, Dr. Paul Stoltz, teaches how to best deal with ANY inevitable adversity that ALL people living on planet earth will face. Your "Adversity Quotient" is a combination of your "Intelligence Quotient", also known as IQ, and your "Emotional Quotient", also known as EQ, which is a combination of your Self Awareness skills, your Self-Management skills, your Social Awareness skills and Social Interaction skills. The formula looks like this: IQ + EQ = AQ. Your AQ (Adversity Quotient) is determined by a number of factors, some of which you have control over, and others are predetermined in your life.

I use the illustration of a tree, which represents your life. The fruit from your own 'tree of life' (the ability to deal well with any adversity that hits you) is rooted in the 'ground' of your background, specifically your genetics, your upbringing as a child, and your faith.

The 'trunk' of your own tree of life is made up of your intelligence, your physical and emotional health, and the character/personality you have developed in your life. The branches that support the fruit of your life are the talents you are blessed with and/or develop, plus the desire you exhibit in improving your life circumstances. Is your tree producing healthy leaves and fruit, or have you gone dormant?

We all know people who have experienced adversity in their lives. Some have packed it in, given up, developed a sense of learned helplessness, began to take a pessimistic view of everything, and lacked the endurance and flexibility to emerge from being a victim. Conversely, we also know people who have developed a sense of empowerment, hardiness, optimism, and resilience who see setbacks as only temporary glitches in their growth as a person. What makes the difference in their lives? It is their Adversity Quotient.

Each person has developed their own personal ability to respond to different stimulus, both negative and positive, via the cognitive psychology of their mind through developing the uniquely human trait of Response-Ability. You can learn how to slow down your response to a negative stimuli, and create a broader assortment of appropriate responses — rather than fight or flight — by learning how to best handle adversity.

The value in learning these models is found in the actual implementation of them in your life. Once I heard and understood the severity of my cancer diagnosis, I applied the C.O.O.R.E. model to my own situation to help myself come up with a course of action.

Control – I knew I had very little control over getting cancer. However, I did have a lot of control over deciding on a course of treatment. I also knew I held the trump card in my recovery plan in that I control my daily attitude!

By learning to control Parkinson's effect on my life, and being in good shape, I knew I could endure the cancer treatments that were suggested.

Origin – I do not know why I developed prostate cancer, but I did learn that cancer likes three things: sugar, increased testosterone, and stress. I decided to adjust my lifestyle to do whatever I could to defeat cancer by modifying my diet, altering the supplements I take, and taking treatments in the early mornings when I am at my strongest mental state. I also endeavored to have more peace, therefore less stress, by trusting God and increasing my faith in Him.

Ownership – I do not believe that I had done anything to cause the cancer, but none the less I had cancer. So, it was important to put together a plan that would facilitate a speedy recovery and be a good example to my family.

Reach – Cancer reaches into every aspect of your life: employment, faith, family, personal attitude, relationships, and many others. I set about making sure I had prayer groups praying for me, updated my will and financial matters, and tried to spend more time with my grandchildren. I also wrote my grandchildren a number of letters on key life topics for them to read at an appropriate time in their lives, in case I was not there to provide grandfatherly wisdom.

Endurance – Unlike Parkinson's, I knew that if we came up with the proper treatment plan and implemented that plan correctly, I could defeat prostate cancer and learn to live with the side effects. The treatments took 45 days and I was told there would be a two-month recovery time from the radiation treatments. I have been monitoring my PSA levels quarterly ever since and I am happy to say I have remained cancer-free!

Regardless of how many Atomic Events you will face in your life, you always have the ability to apply the C.O.O.R.E. model to them and come up with a game plan to effectively deal with each situation.

RISE POINT:
THRIVE DESPITE ADVERSITY

Learning to use and develop a C.O.O.R.E. approach when looking at and dealing with the troubles of life will greatly improve your Adversity Quotient. Additionally, developing your Response-Ability to the Atomic Event in your life by intrinsically following a game plan that includes exercise, intellectual, physical, and spiritual components is critical to thriving despite adversity.

VANTAGE POINT:

LUKE WAALER,
FELLOW PARKIE

My wife was the first person to diagnose me with Parkinson's. At age 48, I didn't expect that to be the explanation for a tremor in my hand or some stiffness in my gait. But she had noticed these things, as well as seeing that my arms didn't swing naturally when I walked.

A quick search on the internet produced a list of common signs of Parkinson's Disease symptoms. As she went down the list, I'd respond with, "Yes, I've got that sign.", or "Nope." Out of 10 or so items, I answered, "Yes" to 7 of them. Together, we started facing the likelihood that I had PD. When an MRI confirmed that I had not experienced a stroke, and the first few doses of carbidopa-levodopa reduced my symptoms, PD became the official diagnosis.

Similar to Greg's experience, the first thing we did was gather all the information we could on Parkinson's Disease to decide what we could control and what we couldn't. In addition to taking the right medication, it seemed exercise played a big role in slowing the progression. I had worked out for most of my life in an effort to keep in shape, but suddenly I had a much stronger incentive. Similar to the scene in *Raiders of the Lost Ark* where Indiana Jones tries to outrun a boulder, I saw exercising as the best way to outrun the effects of PD. I know it'll catch up to me eventually, but the bigger headstart I get, the better off I'll be.

I started taking boxing classes (where I reconnected with Greg after about 25 years), and have recently started taking spin classes for people with PD. Not only does it feel good to exercise, it also helps to know I'm controlling the things that I can control. I still have good days and bad days, but my having some 'internal sense of control' has been a huge help for me.

The righteous person may have many troubles,
but the Lord delivers him from them all.
Psalm 34:19

CHAPTER 5

A LONG-TERM PLAN

MAPPING OUT WHAT IS
MOST IMPORTANT

Summertime in Colorado is an incredibly beautiful season to be outdoors. The powerful runoff from the melting mountain snow brings fly fishing to the forefront of recreational activities. I have always enjoyed fly fishing and even referred to it as my "drug". Standing in a river, watching nature unfold around me, brings on a state of unparalleled peace and joy. Trying to determine what the fish are feeding on by observing the hatch on the river, then presenting the fly that most resembles that hatch, is all part of the strategy for successful fly fishing.

Not long after my PD diagnosis, I went fly fishing hoping to find that place of inner peace. To my dismay, I found I could no longer change flies on my line because of my shaking right hand. Try as I might to keep my hand still, Parkinson's had eliminated the fine motor skills required. So, for a period of three years, I no longer went fly fishing. It was the first formerly joyful activity that I noticed Parkinson's had taken away from me. There are other things like playing basketball and softball that PD also prohibits me from doing. The frustration of not being able to play a sport or participate in activities that I love because of Parkinson's made the devastating effects of my disease seem even worse.

Up to this point in my life, I had always considered myself to be a rock solid individual. My behavioral style put me in leadership roles in most areas of my life. I worked hard to maintain good health and a high fitness level. I pursued success and set challenging goals for myself in all the roles I played. I had often used the analogy of being a rock, but now the rock had a crack in it. Parkinson's Disease symptoms were breaking into every aspect of who I was and what I did.

I realized that I needed to find new activities I could enjoy despite having PD and all the motor and non-motor issues that come with it. This helped me realize I needed a long-term plan to live with purpose. My Internal Locus of Control kicked in and I realized I needed to develop a survival plan. I was beginning to understand I would be in this battle for a long time. I wanted to believe that a cure was just around the corner and I would be back on the water in a matter of months. But the reality is that the discovery of a cure is unlikely to happen in my lifetime.

Every Atomic Event has a lingering impact. As the realization sets in that your life will never fully go back to what it was, it is important to begin to turn your attention forward to things that you can do. A mentor of mine, Harry Wicks, used to tell me, "If you think you can, or if you think you can't, you are right."[15] I needed to come to an understanding of the effects of Parkinson's in a number of roles in my life to establish a plan that could stand the test of time.

For many years I have followed a system of learning to manage the various key roles in my life, which I learned from Kevin McCarthy's book, *The On-*

---

[15] This is a loose version of a quote often ascribed to Henry Ford. *Quote Investigator*. Retrieved 3.4.20 from https://quoteinvestigator.com/2015/02/03/you-can/.

Purpose Person.[16] McCarthy lays out a system designed to help you focus on establishing priorities, first within each role you play in life, then even more important, establishing your priorities among those various roles you have to play. Parkinson's Disease became a new and more urgent reason for me to purposefully examine my goals and strategies for going forward into my challenging future.

McCarthy calls the roles in our lives, "Primary Life Accounts". These "On-Purpose" accounts include the following life roles each person likely has to play:

A. Community/Social
B. Family
C. Financial/Material
D. Life Specific (Other)
E. Mental/Intellectual
F. Physical/Health/Recreation
G. Spiritual
H. Vocational/Career

Tournament of Priorities
Once your On-Purpose life account roles are established, each with their own list of tasks, you must prioritize and pair the tasks against each other, just like sports tournament seeding. All the priorities compete — two at a time — to determine which will advance to the next round. The more priorities identified, the more rounds played until a final winner is crowned in each life role account.

To establish priorities for your On-Purpose Person tournament, start by free-thinking about the things you would like to accomplish for each of the roles in your life role accounts. Many people call this a Bucket List. Write down ten to fifteen individual tasks under each role. They can be short term or long term, individual in nature or group-oriented. They should all be items YOU WANT TO DO. It may take you time to come up

[16] McCarthy, Kevin W. *The On-Purpose Person: Making Your Life Make Sense.* 2009. On Purpose Publishing. Winter Park FL.

with 10-15 items for each role, but if you stop and think about how you actually spend your time or how you would want to spend your time, you will eventually get there.

For example, under my Family account role, I identified the following tasks as being important:

1. Family trip to Kauai for 40th Wedding Anniversary (December 2018) and another to Florida (August 2019)
2. Support my daughters' marriages (financial, love, opportunities to be together, and prayers)
3. Coach grandchildren in a sport
4. Finish writing book, *Rising Above Parkinson's*
5. Write Down "Gregisms" for "A Father's Legacy" book and make scripture scrolls for each
6. Be active in grandchildren's lives (become a watch dog at their school; take them camping, paddle boarding, etc.)
7. Visit my father and help my wife deal with her mother's estate closing
8. Write letters of encouragement to help shed light on life's mysteries for my grandchildren as they grow up
9. Run in races with the grandchildren
10. Fund grandchildren's 529 college accounts
11. Go fishing three times in the summer

Once you have identified the items or important tasks in each life account role, you need to prioritize them and pick the eight that will play in the On-Purpose Tournament. Make your Life Account Bracket by filling in the eight highest ranking tasks. If you've ever participated in a "March Madness Bracket" for the NCAA, you are familiar with"bracket-ology" for the "Road to the Final Four". Honestly rank the 10-15 items you have in each Role by seeding the most important item as the number #1 slot in your bracket. The number #2 slot should be the second most important item in your role, and the third slot #3 should be filled by the third most important item in your Role. Keep doing this until you have your top eight items identified in each or your Life Account Roles.

Items that did not make my family bracket included running in races (the Bolder Boulder) with the grandchildren; funding grandchildren's 529 college funds; and going fishing three times in the summer. But I was able to pick up two of those items in other Life Role Brackets: funding the 529 college funds landed under Financial Role and running a local 10K race (Bolder Boulder) with the entire family under the Recreation Role. That is the beauty of this system; it helps ensure you live an On-Purpose Life throughout all your various roles

Next, fill in your tournament bracket by seeding your Number #1 item against your Number #8 item; your Number #2 item against your Number #7; your Number #3 against your Number #6; and your Number #4 against your #5 items.

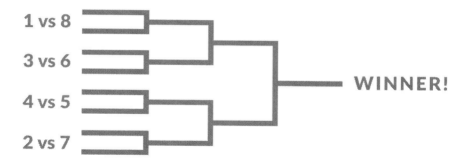

My family bracket for 2019 ended up looking like this:

#1 (family trip) beat #8 (letters of encouragement) – Who wouldn't want to go to Kauai? Besides I would not get to 41 years of marriage if we had not gone!

#6 (active in grandchildren's lives) beats #3 (coach grandchildren) – I have coached my grandchildren in various sports for years. However, by being involved in many more aspects of my grandchildren's lives I will have more opportunities to help them in life.

#5 ("Gregisms") beats #4 (finish writing book) — Passing on the wisdom of my life, to each of them on an individual basis, is way more important to my grandchildren than any book about my battles with Parkinson's.

#2 (support daughters' marriages) beats #7 (help aging parents) — Closing out my in-laws estate properly is important, but supporting my daughters throughout the issues of their lives is critical. Proverbs 22:6 says, *Train up a child in the way he should go, and when he is old he will not depart from it.*

Now, playing out the bracket to the end gets even harder because everything remaining is very important:

#6 (be active in grandchildren's lives) beats #1 (family trip) — We have been on many Family trips (it is one reason we are such a tight family) but being involved in my grandchildren's lives during this season of my life is priceless.

#5 ("Gregisms") beats #2 (support daughters' marriages) — Both involve passing on wisdom to the grandchildren, but the day-in and day-out impact of being a source of guidance in their lives is immeasurable. Additionally, it takes pressure off of my daughter's lives!

Finally, the championship of the Family bracket goes to #6 (active in grandchildren's lives). It is important to my wife and I to be active in our grandchildren's lives. Neither of us had much interaction with our grandparents and we do not want to short change our grandchildren. As I walked through the Tournament of Prorities based on my family roles, it created clarity and emphasis for the time and resources in my life.

Identifying Important Tasks
While some of the priorities in an area are based on a simple desire to do them, others may come about through hardship or a situation you

are faced with. In my case, the decision to prioritize staying active in my grandchildren's lives came about from an experience with my grandson. My second oldest grandson, aged seven at the time, became fearful of going to his first-grade class because the other children were teasing him about his food allergies.

It got so bad that his parents were frustrated and wondered what to do. Along comes grandpa with an idea. What if I take him to school to cut down on the separation anxiety? That idea worked on the first day, probably because it was a Friday and he was looking forward to the weekend. But then Monday rolled around and my grandson didn't even want to get in the car to go to school with me.

Time for some grandpa wisdom. My grandson has always liked necklaces, and I have worn a golden cross necklace since college (1976). The next day when I went to pick up my grandson, I took off my cross necklace and told him to wear it to school. I told him, "Every time you feel an anxiety attack coming on, grab hold of the cross and think about your favorite times with your grandparents and know that Jesus is watching over you."

He was very aware of the significance of the cross necklace to me — and though he still is a work in progress — now he has a chart for good behavior, and he earns stars for each day he is able to manage his anxiety. I realized that being there for him really mattered. It also cost me half the price of a new paddle board as a reward for earning 5 stars through his daily successes, but that is a small price to pay in the long run. This experience of helping my grandson with his anxiety made me realize that my original seeding of being active in my grandchildren's lives at #6, was actually more important than any of the other seven tasks.

Mapping Out Your Own Tournament
Now that you see how each role has its own tournament, do this seeding exercise for each of the roles (Family, Vocation, etc.) in your life. If you spread out the eight different life accounts on a table, you will quickly see which tasks on your tournaments appear in two or more accounts.

These are the bucket list items you are most inclined to achieve. Each life account bracket eventually crowns a champion task or item. The really interesting tournament to play is the Tournament of Champions. Every item in this bracket is a top priority in some phase of your life, but there can only be one true champion that you want to focus on.

The champions of my eight Priority Tournaments based on all my life roles were seeded in the following manner for the Quarter Finals:

A. **Community/Social:** (#1) Help create and fund Parkinson's Pointe
B. **Family:** (#6) Be Active in Grandchildren's Lives
C. **Financial/Material:** (#4) Buy a Beach Home with Cash
D. **Life Specific:** (#8) Disciplined Prayer Life
E. **Mental/Intellectual:** (#3) Write *Rising Above Parkinson's* book
F. **Physical/Health:** (#2) Live a Lifestyle to Thrive
G. **Spiritual:** (#5) Teach God's Word and Faith
H. **Vocational/Career:** (#7) Manage Retirement Funds Correctly

My tournament played out with (A. Parkinson's Pointe) playing (E. *Rising Above Parkinson's* book); (G. Teach Faith) playing (F. Lifestyle to thrive) in the Semi Finals, then (A. Parkinson's Pointe) playing (G. Teach Faith) in the Championship match. In my world, helping to create and build a Parkinson's Community Center such as Parkinson's Pointe would be a significant accomplishment, but Teaching God's Word and Faith — at every opportunity — is the Great Commission in life.

It is important to remember that the On-Purpose Person Tournament is something you should do every year, as your life ebbs and flows, and the situations of your life unfold. I also believe that it is important for couples (if applicable) to write out their On-Purpose Tournaments separately. Then get together (a great excuse for a weekend get-a-way) to discuss what is growing in importance to each other, so that you continue to grow towards each other.

MODEL:
THE IMPORTANCE OF ROLE MODELS

While I mapped out my own On-Purpose Person Tournaments to help me focus on where to expend my energy, I also needed to look for a role model — someone who had lived a full life despite having to deal with an Atomic Event. I didn't have to look far. Looking around in my sphere of relationships, I have a great friend, Steve. He is a Christian, is athletic, and one of the most astute businessmen I know. He is also a recovering alcoholic who has not had a drink in more than 25 years. I picked his brain to find out what he thought was the secret to such a successful run while dealing with such a hard issue as alcoholism. He had several pieces of advice to share with me:

1. Sometimes you need to hit rock bottom before you can "Look up".
2. It is Steve's personal "choice" to not drink anymore.
3. A lifetime of sobriety is lived "One day at a time".

You will not meet a more likable person than Steve. He is very involved in his church and volunteers for several community upgrading organizations that repair homes and rebuild forgotten communities. I have worked on community fix-up projects with Steve in Colorado, around the US, and several foreign countries. He is the type of quiet leader that people naturally gravitate toward. He never makes you feel out of your league, even though you might not have a clue of how to fix plumbing, remove flooring, or put in new drywall!

Steve did not come from a great family background, but he has not let that deter him from living a significant life. If we go back to the C.O.O.R.E. model, Steve did not have a lot of Control over his family situation, and the origin of his alcoholic behavior certainly came from his parents and siblings. What has turned Steve's life around is his ability to take

Ownership of his addiction, and not let the ramifications of that lifestyle reach out and ruin the rest of his life or his family's. His ability to take life "One day at a time" gives him endurance. He is a beacon of light to many people around him to help them get through their Atomic Event.

RISE POINT:
PREPARE YOUR ARK

There is a strategy for preparedness that is known as the Noah Principle. It is not your ability to predict rain that counts, it is your ability to have prepared an Ark. In other words, you cannot predict what might happen to you. My experience using the On-Purpose Person strategies prepared me for getting back out on the water in new ways.

VANTAGE POINT:

STEVE WURST,
LONG-TIME FRIEND

"God doesn't waste the hurts from our past. Instead, He uses them for great things." This is a saying that I have long lived by.

I met Greg Ritscher in November of 1990. He came to work with me at a wholesale distribution company selling supplies to landscape and irrigation contractors. When we first met, one of our discussions was about the products and services we provide to our clients. Greg did not know the first thing about any of the products that we sold, but that did not deter him one bit. His energy and thirst for knowledge was just one of the appealing qualities I saw in Greg. His love of sports and his competitive nature were attributes I also shared and valued. One of his greatest assets is his strong Christian faith. I have never been around someone who openly shares their love of God as often as Greg does.

I can still remember the day, April 26th of 2011, I received a phone call from Greg letting me know he was just returning from a doctor's appointment and had been diagnosed with Parkinson's Disease. I was stunned! I wanted to make sure I had heard him correctly; but unfortunately, I had. I will remember that phone call forever. We had a short conversation that day and many more to follow. I will never truly understand why this is happening to my friend.

As Greg mentioned previously in this chapter, I am and will forever be a recovering alcoholic. One of the important lessons I have learned in rehab and AA is when you find yourself in a hole: QUIT DIGGING! But Greg had not dug this hole. To my knowledge, he has never done anything to deserve his Parkinson's diagnosis. That is the funny (not so funny) way that God uses our lives to help us serve others. Greg has been that servant. Greg tells me that through the Parkinson's Association, he has been asked to help others who have reached out with questions. Greg is always willing to offer wise counsel and be candid yet encouraging with the new members joining his special "Parkie" club.

Since day one, Greg has attacked his diagnosis with a competitive spirit. He has read everything he can get his hands on, participated in every study he can get into, and listened to or talked with every doctor or speaker he can find on this subject. Greg has used his faith as a shield to keep his thoughts positive when others, like me, cannot understand how he is patient with and encouraging to his family and friends who do not comprehend his situation. He has utilized exercise to keep his thoughts strong and his body even stronger than when I first met him almost 30 years ago.

Greg talks about the big problem/little problems "squares" (discussed in *Chapter Eight*) and what he can see, as well as what others see. Greg has consistently asked me over the years about what changes I have noticed in his actions, behaviors, and mannerisms. He has warned me about traits of Parkinson's; what to watch for with idiosyncrasies caused by the drugs he takes, such as impulsiveness. For example, if he called me up and wanted to go buy a boat, I would have to tell him I am the wrong person to ask, since I would probably pick him up and go help him buy the boat. He has never done that, but I keep waiting. Greg has always asked if I have noticed differences in him from year-to-year. As hard as it is for me to honestly tell him what I have observed, Greg takes the information and uses it to work on bettering himself, prolonging his life, or investigating a medication to ease the symptoms.

Just as I will never be a recovered alcoholic, Greg will never recover from Parkinson's. What Greg will do — in my opinion — is make everyone he has come into contact with, or will come in contact with, a better person. And not just Parkinson patients but all his family, friends, and acquaintances. I am a better person since the day Greg came into my life! I know many people feel the same way.

Listen to advice and accept discipline, and at the end
you will be counted among the wise. Many are the plans in a
person's heart, but it is the Lord's purpose that prevails.
Proverbs 19:20-21

CHAPTER 6

DRAFTING A TEAM

IF YOU WANT TO GO FAR,
GO TOGETHER

Often quoted, but with no apparent authoritative citation, an African proverb states, "If you want to go fast, go alone. If you want to go far, go together." One of my mentors when I was young, taught me Proverbs 15:22 which states, *Plans fail for lack of counsel, but with many advisers they succeed.*

After my diagnosis, one of the first things I knew I had to do was put together a support team to help me battle Parkinson's. Finding people I could count on to help me through this battle was critical to the remainder of my life. I knew I could count on my wife, over 40 years of marriage and raising a family ensured me of that. I am a very open person with my life, and I knew I had to tell my children, friends, mentors, co-workers, and Bible study classmates I was in for a difficult trip. I needed all the wise counsel I could get.

I have played competitive team sports all of my life. A good group of athletes with a common goal, playing to each other's strengths as a team, will always be the best setup to win. I needed to put the best, most cohesive support team together that I could, to try to win over the long haul against Parkinson's. I will use a baseball team analogy for the structure of my PD support team.

The most important position on my team is the catcher because they call all of the pitches for the pitcher (me). My wife fills the catcher role perfectly. She knows all of my pitch capabilities and tendencies. More importantly, she knows how I handle pressure situations. Her love and counsel has helped guide my life since we married in 1978. I trust her wisdom and understanding of me, even when I am having a bad day with symptoms. She is the love of my life!

Up the middle, I have my daughters and sons-in-law to turn double plays at second base; and a group of friends to play the hot corner at third base. They know my tendencies and are a great sounding board for watching my progression with the disease because I see them regularly. My personal mentor will play first base and hold the runners on, like when he holds me accountable for my actions. Strong people of faith from my church and Bible studies will patrol the outfield and track down any mistakes I make while pitching. Not only will they hold me accountable for my actions, but they are also a strong component of my prayer team.

I am fortunate as a Parkie to have a very strong team, which I have developed over the years. But what if you are not so well supported?

You can build a network via service providers and Parkinson's associations. Finding a good support group is an invaluable source of both educational and social assistance. Whatever you do, do not try to take on your Atomic Event by yourself! I know how you feel: you think you are becoming a burden to your team. Instead, think of the joy that your support team can feel knowing they are helping you thrive.

I also knew that I had to further develop my network with additional services and providers. These needs included: medical insurance (which we were changing at work), doctors, a financial planner (turns out he has Parkinson's, too), gym and yoga instructors, Parkinson's support group leaders, and a Movement Specialist Physical Therapist.

I wanted to have a team watching out for me, from all perspectives. They would hold me accountable regarding my efforts and attitude so that I could chart the course I would take to thrive in the balance of my life. You quickly learn who your friends are — and who are merely acquaintances — while you are going through an Atomic Event.

As an example, my movement specialist has an uplifting way of starting and ending our sessions. She calls them "Victories". At the beginning of each session she asks me to identify new challenges I can tackle that I did not attempt prior to having Parkinson's. We review the notes from our previous sessions, especially the goals I set for myself, to see how I am progressing. She challenged me to climb one 14,000' mountain per year. This past year in August, I climbed Pikes Peak — a 14,115 foot high mountain — with my son-in-law, Lindo. I had to train to get ready to accomplish my goal, which was just as important as the actual climb. By achieving victories in my training during June and July, the actual climb in August went very smoothly.

Adversity is not evenly distributed throughout your life. Walt Disney was wrong; in some stories you do not "live happily ever after". Grief over losing your old, former NORMAL LIFE is a deeply personal feeling. Yet the human spirit has a strong capacity to be resilient and persevere. Just ask anyone who has been abducted, lived through the hell of losing a spouse or child, or survived the Holocaust. That is why I read Victor Frankl's writings; he lived through Auschwitz!

The Adversity Quotient is where your IQ (intelligence quotient) plus your EQ (emotional quotient) plays a large part in teaching you how to handle adversity in your life. It is one thing to be intelligent, but it is entirely a different thing to know how to use that intelligence properly and in an appropriate manner. I believe they call that "wisdom" or properly applied intelligence. Learning how to deal with adversity, and develop the strength to nurture the power of resilience in both ourselves and our loved ones, is a life skill we should all focus on. Could you give them a better gift for life? The following model is one way you might find to improve your resilience factor.

MODEL:
THE THREE P'S BY MARTIN SELIGMAN

Psychologist Martin Seligman[17] developed the Three P's of how adversity, and your response to it, can stunt or delay your recovery from grief. The first P is for Personalization. We blame ourselves for not doing or saying something to prevent the tragic event. Thoughts like, "I should not have let him drive the car" or, "I never should have let him start rock climbing". This is where the C for Control and O for Ownership in the C.O.O.R.E. model comes into play. Anyone can beat themselves up for any decision made with a high level of uncertainty attached to it, but will that create progress?

Over-personalizing your decisions in the past will certainly impede your resilience factor in life. For a time, my wife's profession involved taking groups on 10- to 14-day-long mission trips in the summers. My daughters would cope well for the first week, but after that they would start to get grouchy, so I would take them on various 'road trips'. We packed our bags, got in the car, and just decided spontaneously where to go. The mountains, National Parks (like Yellowstone), and beaches were favorite destinations.

One time — as my daughters were getting older — they all wanted to bring friends on our road trip. My daughter (then in high school) wanted

[17] Seligman, Martin. "3 Ps." *Growing Resilient.* Retrieved 12.1.19 from growingresilient.com/home/tools/3-ps/.

to bring a male friend from one of her sports teams with us. I knew the kid, so I agreed. Well you can guess where this is going, and sure enough my daughter was involved in a date rape-type situation. It took four years of intense therapy for my daughter to get beyond this Atomic Event in her life, and I am glad to say she is a lovely, vibrant woman today!

If I hadn't known about personalization and not blaming myself for ever bringing up road trips or allowing a boy to come with us, I am not sure I would have survived that family Atomic Event. My experience taught me a number of valuable life lessons which I have shared with other fathers. They faced similar issues and heard me speak about trying to build resilience into our lives.

The second P is for Pervasiveness. We believe that the effects of the Atomic Event will last forever and invade every aspect of our lives. Thoughts flood our minds such as, "I will never be happy again", or "I can never look at the mountains again". This is where the skill set of dealing with O for Origin and R for Reach in the C.O.O.R.E model matter the most. Trust me, while we were living through those four years of living hell as my daughter processed that event, I was reminded of my decision every day!

Finally, the third P is for Permanence. We feel that the negative outcome to the event will last forever. We believe that for the rest of our lives, the aftershocks of the Atomic Event will permeate our hearts and minds. "I can never forgive the drunk driver", or " I hope that the cheat rots in hell!". This is where the skill set of forgiveness can set us free from being a prisoner, giving us E for Endurance in the C.O.O.R.E. model. Time moves on; so does life. One of my best friends (I was Best Man at his wedding), died suddenly at an early age. It was so tough to deal with! I think of him often, and it still hurts to do so. The memories I have of him are more treasured now than if he were still with us.

Resilience can be defined as improving the speed and strength of our recovery from an adverse condition or affect. Victor Frankl wrote about it in his book, *Man's Search for Meaning*. He observed that Holocaust prisoners who lived beyond the camps were able to find a meaning in life, despite their former or present condition, and they did not depend on traditional human instincts of psychoanalytic psychiatry.

Resilience in life can be learned through forgiveness and a positive outlook. Victor Frankl called it "The last ultimate freedom". We can choose to respond to any type of experience or treatment in any way we choose. The prisoners who lived did not return hate for hate with the guards. Instead, they choose to forgive and expand their view of "hardiness", or the ability to endure difficult conditions. The key point is that it is an internal, personal decision, which everyone is capable of.

Parkinson's disease has a wide assortment of disaffects on your body. It's like a menu of things that go wrong or a "cafeteria" of negative symptoms you get to pick from. That is why I suggest you look for the positive things in your new life with Parkinson's and not focus on what you cannot do. Do not let the Three P's rob you of elasticity in your approach to life. We all make decisions in life we later regret. Keep moving forward; stay positive; remember you have Response-Ability!

RISE POINT:
BUILD A SUPPORT NETWORK

Do not try to take on Parkinson's without help. Develop a support team that includes family and friends. Build a strong support network of providers and services who will work WITH you. There is power in numbers. Do not let the Three P's drag you down. Look for Victories in your life with Parkinson's and learn the power of Resilience to sustain you. The stronger support team and network you put together, the better equipped you will be to take on a beast like Parkinson's!

VANTAGE POINT:

COURTNEY RITSCHER MOORE,
DAUGHTER

My father, Greg Ritscher, has always been a source of strength and guidance in my life. I reflect on my wedding day with fondness, remembering the dancing, antics, and the overwhelming love of two families coming together across the continents. I had never expected to marry a man from Australia, just as I had never expected my health-conscious father to be diagnosed with an incommunicable, incurable disease like Parkinson's.

Anyone faced with such an Atomic Event can readily spiral into despair or hopelessness. I believe my father has set a great example for me: I do not need to be happy about the circumstances I may face, but I can control my reaction to those circumstances. Can I be sad? Yes! Can I be angry? Of course! Can I also be gracious, forgiving, and hopeful? Yes!

I feel being faced with a disease that is presently misunderstood, gives anyone living with it the power to find their own coping mechanisms with less judgment or pressure than a disease which is well understood. People living with Parkinson's have the chance to influence not only their own lives, but they can support others by participating in research and through exploring what alleviates their own symptoms day-to-day.

From my youth, I have enjoyed yoga. This interest was met with some skepticism from my parents when I was younger. However, after my father's diagnosis, this paradigm has shifted tremendously. Now, practicing yoga with my father is something we both look forward to. For each of us, it is time to connect with one's body, nervous system (no matter what condition a doctor tells you it is in), and more importantly, with oneself.

My father has been diagnosed with Parkinson's, but he remains my father. He remains wonderful and loved. Amazingly, he is now a far kinder and gentler person to those around him.

My two messages to anyone reading this are: "You are not your illness." and, "You are not your painful past!" We all possess a fabulous, inherent, changeable quality which is new every moment. We can choose life. We can choose to be gracious with ourselves and with others. Never be afraid to explore how vast your life experience can be or how any diagnosis may open up new perspectives.

Your greatest companion is with you in every adventure life presents; it's you!

Plans fail for lack of counsel, but with many advisers they succeed.
Proverbs 15:22

CHAPTER 7

WHAT TO DO NEXT

WHAT TO DO,
AND WHAT NOT TO DO

"Now what?" That is exactly what I remember thinking after being hit with each Atomic Event in my life. The "Now what?" was on my mind clear back in my college days, especially after graduating. I had always been a proactive person, as well as goal-oriented. So, before my last year in college began, I sat down and came up with a game plan. I still have the note card on which I wrote my goals for my senior year at the University of Colorado: "get my degree with at least a 3.0 GPA, find a good job using the resources at CU's Career Placement Center, and find a wife in the college co-ed gene pool". Maybe it sounds too pragmatic, but that is how I think!

The reason I needed to stay above 3.0 in my grade point average at CU was based on a deal my father made with me. If I kept my GPA above 3.0 in Business Administration, and graduated in four years, he would pay 100% of my college costs (in the 1970's that was approximately $15,000.00). My father taught me a great life lesson in how he treated and motivated each of his children. He treated us individually, not always equally. He tried to influence each of us based upon our needs and talents. He behaved very similar to the Master in the Parable of the Talents found in Matthew 25, starting with verse 15. He understood that our talents were varied, that our abilities and drives were all unique, and so he tailored his expectations accordingly.

As far as finding a good job, I graduated in May of 1978 just when the economy was picking back up after a fairly severe recession through the mid-1970's. I knew I needed to use the Career Placement Services (this was pre-internet time) to get exposure to major companies that were hiring managers. As you were allowed to choose three firms to interview with, I ended up selecting Armstrong World Industries, The Boy Scouts of America, and the United States Secret Service. I was hired by the folks at Armstrong, spent six years with them, before moving back to Colorado to start raising a family.

Back in 1978, you used to have to get up at 5 am on Monday mornings during the winter interviewing months and walk to the Career Placement Center on campus. Then, stand in a line to sign up for job interviews with your favored companies on a clipboard, all on a first come, first served basis. Needless to say, you missed a lot of good companies to interview with due to this archaic system. Some companies were known for great interviews and highly valued to interview with, when their hiring managers were on campus.

One of these companies was a multinational cooperation that I will refer to as "Company X". They were known for their high-pressure interviews and IF you could make an impression with them, you could make an impression on anyone! I badly wanted to interview with them, if only for the experience. Sadly, all their interview slots were filled by the time I got the clipboard. They had been in the news just prior to being on campus because one of their battery factories in India had exploded, killing hundreds of people.

I was a Resident Advisor in CU's dormitory system, and one of the ladies on my floor worked at the Career Placement Center as a secretary. On the one day Company X was in town for interviews, it snowed heavily, and the first person on the schedule had to cancel their interview time because of the weather. That secretary called me (on my rotary dialed, land-line phone), by chance catching me in my room. She said if I ran over I could get an interview with the Company X hiring manager. I arrived — breathing heavily with snow in my hair — just in time for the first interview of the day.

I walked into the room with my resume in hand, gave it to the hiring manager — who was sitting behind an elevated desk (to show power) — and I was told to sit down. The manager never looked at me. With my file directly in front of his face he stated, "Mr. Ritscher, it is hot in this room; please open the window".

It was more of a command than a request. I went to the only window in the room — a single pane, wood framed style — on the ground level of the building, and I found that the window was screwed shut. I told the hiring manager the window had been screwed shut, probably for the winter weather and because it was so old, and it couldn't be opened. His response was to state, "This interview cannot begin until you open the window, Mr. Ritscher!" Again, I mentioned that the window was screwed shut and without tools it could not be opened. I returned to my seat, beneath his desk.

The manager just sat there and said nothing for several minutes. Finally, I asked if we were going to have an interview. He then stated I had not lived up to the criteria required of me to have an interview with Company X. I told him it was impossible to open the window as it was screwed shut. He said, "Once you live up to the criteria required of you, I will be happy to start the interview." I had grown tired of the "Jedi Knight mind tricks" and the interviewer's arrogance. So I stood up, picked up my chair, and threw it through the window!

The sound of broken glass brought many people rushing to the room, and the hiring manager said, "What in the hell are you doing?" I told him I was making sure Company X could not use such a childish power ploy on any other University of Colorado Business School candidates that day. I grabbed my resume and left. I never heard from anyone at the Career Placement Center regarding the incident, and Company X was soon out of business. While their closure was not because of me, I did feel I certainly had my say.

As far as finding a wife goes, I am one of the luckiest men alive. I was not a big "dater" in high school or college. As a child, I had a medical issue with drainage in my ears and had to undergo four different operations by the time I was five. My parents made the decision to start me in grade school a year ahead of time, thinking that I would be held back at some point dealing with these medical issues. When I was in second grade, science developed a wonder drug that cleared up my ear drainage issue but it had the side effect of delaying and stunting my growth. Between these two factors, when I graduated from high school, I was just under five feet tall and weighed just over 100 lbs. I was the size of a fifth grader. I swore I would never date anyone taller than I was, so I didn't have too many young ladies to choose from.

Against my parent's will, I took a year off between high school and college to let my body catch up to my age. I grew 10 inches that year, and though my clothes always looked like they did not fit right, I matured in several ways during that time.

In my junior year of college, I was again a Resident Advisor, assigned to a coed floor. I had finally started to date a couple of ladies. One of them, my future wife, lived with the sister of my roommate, so I saw her at least one time a month as brother and sister would share care packages from home. At the beginning of my senior year on Labor Day weekend, we went on our first date as part of a dorm excursion to a local amusement park. We had a great time. She was a Christian, cute as a bug, and as spunky as they come.

We dated throughout the fall semester, but it wasn't until an intramural broomball game (ice hockey without skates) that I was sure I wanted to marry her. It was a playoff game and in the midst of a wild scrum in front of our goal, I was yelling for our defenders to hit the ball to the side. Phylis, my future wife, stole the ball from an attacker. She started to hit it towards center ice while I was yelling for it on the side boards. She stopped mid-swing, put her hands on her hips and told me — in no uncertain terms — to shut up and quit telling people what to do! One of the opponents, seeing an opportunity to steal the ball, ran over to swipe the ball away. Phylis whirled around, pointed her finger at the young man and said, "Don't you dare touch the ball!"

He froze in his tracks. The play stopped and the referee came over and asked Phylis if we were done having an argument, and would it be alright if we started playing again? Phylis said she was tired of listening to me telling her what to do, and she was not going to play anymore. No one else in my life had ever throttled me like that. I knew right then that I wanted those genes in my offspring. Just kidding, but I was impressed by her authority and spunk! We started dating seriously after that event, and married in December of 1978. What a blessed man I am.

What Not to Do
It can be easy to develop an attitude of "learned helplessness" from your PD support team. In an effort to help you, support team members sometimes overstep their boundaries and try to do too much for you. This might include chauffeuring you around, running your errands, or the like. You are still able to do these things yourself, maybe with a bit of struggle, but letting them take over is an easy trap to fall into.

I call it, "Playing the Parkinson's trump card". I will selfishly tell my wife one of my non-motor (unseen) symptoms is bothering me and that I want to go home to rest (to watch a game on TV) instead of going to brunch with friends and having to interact with a lot of people. You have to be cognizant of this "crying wolf" behavior.

I want to control my destiny in life by attempting to think ahead of various scenarios. This allows me to be in a position to move in any direction I need based on the events actually unfolding. This is called an 'internal locus of control'. It is considered internal because I am trying to control events with my own thinking. But don't kid yourself, you DO NOT have tangible control over what course your life will ultimately take, though you can choose your attitude and you can be well prepared for a variety of events that are likely.

The opposite of this behavior is to have an 'external locus of control'. This is much more common among people with Parkinson's disease. This is where you let everyone else make all your key decisions for you. It is easy to think that doctors or physical therapists — with all their training and certification — know everything and you should not question them. This is especially true in the case of prescription drugs and therapy options. I encourage you to ask questions to maintain an internal locus of control.

No matter what your Atomic Event is in your life, remember you have the ability to respond to the stimuli any way you want. Whether it was getting married, having children, or hearing I had Prostate Cancer in 2016, I have tried to study and prepare for the proper response to dramatic events in my life. The prostate cancer event reinforced in my mind what one of my mentors in life, Harry Wicks, used to tell me, "Chance favors the prepared mind." I took that to mean because I had already experienced my PD prognosis and had always stayed in great shape, I was able to hear the "C" word and still think we could come up with a workable solution. Once I was over the shock, I would "cowboy up" and start an aggressive treatment plan to kill the cancer, pronto!

When I look back, I see how learning to handle my Parkinson's and prostate cancer has taught me an invaluable life lesson. It's called the Theory of Residual Uncertainty. I learned this at an early age and applied it to my Parkinson's diagnosis. All during my high school and college years I was blessed with Harry Wicks as my mentor. We went to the same church and he was the youth-group leader for high school kids.

Ancient philosophers had a saying, "When the student is ready, the teacher will appear!"[18] That is exactly what happened in my life with Harry. He was a bright, young entrepreneur with a beautiful wife. He owned his own company that focused on computer-based training (this was in the early 1970's so that in itself was a rarity). Harry was not only instrumental in maturing my faith, but he also taught me many of the models I have lived my life by including the Theory of Residual Uncertainty and the On Purpose Person.

His greatest lesson for my life, however, was what I learned while watching such a strong Christian man succumb to his own cancer with a positive attitude. He made a lasting impact on many people's lives. I owe it to Harry to live out the balance of my life in the same way he faced his death. I am sure he is in Heaven watching over me.

Harry believed in the Theory of Residual Uncertainty (TRU).[19] This theory was devised to aid in strategic business decision making by framing the factors of uncertainty into four distinct category levels. TRU says that at any given time there are always some factors in your life that are causing uncertainty. We live in an age of radical, discontinuous change. Uncertainty is not only present in our lives, it is proliferating. Uncertainty is not merely the dark counterpart to what is knowable; it always involves risk, yet it always offers opportunity as well.

MODEL:
THEORY OF RESIDUAL UNCERTAINTY

Theory of Residual Uncertainty is all environmental influences interacting in your life over time, minus the relevant factors of your life values and

[18] Wilder, Bill. "When the Student is Ready, the Teacher Will Appear". 2013. *Industry Week.* Retrieved 1.2.20 from industryweek.com/leadership/change-management/article/22009744/when-the-student-is-ready-the-teacher-will-appear.
[19] Courtney, Hugh; Kirkland, Jane; Viguerie, Patrick. "Strategy Under Uncertainty". November 1997. *Hbr.* Retrieved 12.7.19 from https://hbr.org/1997/11/strategy-under-uncertainty.

beliefs, which leaves you with a residual amount of uncertainty that is always present in your life. The passage of time helps to clear present residual uncertainty (What will the stock market do today?), but it also brings new levels of uncertainty with it (What will the market do tomorrow?). Uncertainty is determined by many factors — some of which are known better than others — multiplied by the relative probability for each scenario to happen, including key trigger events.

Using the stock market example, you choose stocks based on your knowledge and values, but you do not know what economic, political, or natural influences will appear on any given day. As the day progresses, new factors come into play and your stock's value changes every minute of the day. Once the trading day is over, you compare the stock price at the end of the day to the price at the beginning of the day. You can analyze all the factors that impacted the price on that day, but that does not mean those same factors will have the same impact the next day. There is always a residual amount of uncertainty with the ownership of your stock.

There are four levels of TRU:

Level Four:
Highest level of Uncertainty – Future outcomes are both unknown and unknowable. True Ambiguity. Limitless number of possibilities. You cannot identify relevant variables or "Customers/Competitors" to monitor. There are 360 degrees of possible outcomes.

Level Three:
Upper-range Uncertainty – You can identify a range of possible outcomes. Trigger events, critical variables, and dynamic paths appear. "Customers/ Competitors" appear on the horizon but are indistinguishable. Small, quick pilot programs can provide some insight. Assessing the payoffs of various scenarios playing out then shows which variables have the largest impact on the most scenarios. This now looks like 180 degrees of possible outcomes.

Level Two:
Mid-range Uncertainty – Distinct possible outcomes can be identified. Trigger events are better known, however "Customers/Competitors" responses are still unpredictable. You need to assess how each strategy changes the probability of a positive outcome. You can analyze the risk/return for each ploy, using "known" information. Either "A" or "B"; but maybe "C", if "X" happens. This now looks like there are three possible outcomes, each of which is dependent on factor "X". There are now just 90 degrees of possible outcomes.

Level One:
Lowest-level Uncertainty – Now a clear enough path is identified, because most factors are known. "Customers/Competitors" reactions are predictable. You can choose a strategy that maximizes the payoff. Uncertainty of this scenario is low, but now you need to watch for new trigger events. There are only 45 degrees of possible outcomes.

When I heard the words, "You have Parkinson's Disease", that put me directly at Level Four TRU.

Parkinson's at Level Four:
What is Parkinson's Disease? How did I get it? Did I do something wrong? Will it kill me? Who should I tell, and what should I tell them? How do I tell someone about something I do not know about? Is there a cure? How is this going to impact my: Marriage? Children? Employment? Future plans? Uncertainty about my condition affected everything in my life.

Parkinson's at Level Three:
Then, with the passage of time, I quickly assessed my resources: I needed to select a doctor and I needed to select a pharmacological plan. Are there specialists in this field? What will my insurance cover? Who wants to help? Are there support groups? Do I want to take part in research studies? As the answers to these and other factors became known, my path became more clear.

Parkinson's at Level Two:
Once I started to go to Parkinson's symposiums, I learned about the different specialists. I narrowed down my choices of doctors to work with based on their views of drugs, exercise, diet, and bedside manner. Then the environment shifted, and my health insurance carrier changed at work. So, now I had to decide if I would just pay for my treatment expenses via my HSA or use the insurance companies list of doctors. But the choices of which path to take became much clearer.

Parkinson's at Level One:
I realized I liked working with doctors who are more homeopathic and take a whole-person perspective. Time had gone by and I learned that doctors and pharmaceuticals are just one part of my treatment plan. Boxing, diet, exercise, physical therapy, participating in research studies, and yoga are all key parts to my support system. I have found a way to make Parkinson's disease a "positive" in my life by meeting with newly diagnosed people, speaking to support groups, using research honorariums to build up my grandsons' 529 college fund, and just becoming a "kinder, gentler person" (my daughter's words).

In summary, I have been blessed beyond belief to have had Phylis, my wife, and Harry, a mentor, introduced into my life to help prepare me for the many uncertain events that have come my way.

RISE POINT:
WHAT TO DO

If you apply some of the principles of TRU to your situation, you should be able to pass through the four levels at a faster and smoother pace, while maximizing the positive outcome. Access your resources: family, doctors, finances, insurance, support groups. But above all, access your attitude! Proverbs 17:22 states, *A cheerful heart is good medicine, but a crushed spirit dries up the bones.*

VANTAGE POINT:

CANDACE PEDRAZA,
DAUGHTER

There are very few days in my life where I remember exactly where I was, what I was doing, the clothes I was wearing, and the way the sun was hitting the floor. September 11, 2001 is one of them. The day my dear friend Edmund died was another. And I know with certainty I will always remember the day, even the moment, when I heard that my Dad was diagnosed with Parkinson's Disease.

After the initial diagnosis, we all went into a research mode to try to understand the disease in preparing ourselves for what may lie ahead. The words "degenerative" and "no cure" stand out in my mind from those early days. The more I learned about Parkinson's Disease, the more I understood just how terrible and life altering it was going to be for my Dad and, ultimately, our family. I pictured my Mom in a few short years (or longer if we were lucky) helping my father into a wheelchair and him not recognizing her.

I began to understand the strength that would be required not only for my father as he degrades but more so for my mother. As a married woman myself without any children at the time, I knew that my timeline for having kids was going to have to be expedited beyond what we had planned. I couldn't picture a life where my children didn't know and love my father. Also living across the country from my parents at that time, made the geographical distance between us seem even more vast as I continued to delve into research regarding Parkinson's Disease.

Understanding what will come next can sometimes bring comfort, even under seemingly terrible circumstances. As an Enneagram 8,[20] like my father, control is highly important to me. This research phase helped me to understand and even master the disease in my mind. That gave my heart the space it needed to feel the incredibly intense emotions associated with a big diagnosis. I tend to live out my life ten years ahead of myself, as my husband likes to point out. Running hypothetical situations through my mind meant that if and when those moments arrived, I would be that much more prepared.

It's funny what we do to pretend we have some sort of control over uncontrollable situations like these. It's in those moments I find that falling on my knees and listening to a never changing, mighty, and good God can have the most powerful impact on what is to come next.

What's interesting is that every single human being on the planet is only guaranteed one common experience from their moment of conception: death. Not everyone gets to be raised in a certain country. Many don't have family support. Others will never come to know about Jesus Christ. Some aren't even given the opportunity to even be born alive. Not everyone goes through the same hardships. However, without a doubt, every person alive now — or who was in the past or will be in the future — can count death as a commonality. I always wonder why we fear it the way we do in our culture?

Death wasn't something that I was very familiar with until recent years. I was blessed to have lived as long as I did until I experienced the loss of a dear friend when I was 22-years-old. And another when I was 26. And losing our first child when I was age 27. And another friend when I was 28. And now the deaths of older members of our family into my 30's. I don't fear death the way that I used to. It is and always will be tragic, but how we respond may be the greatest contribution we make to God's kingdom here on earth.

---

[20] "The Nine Enneagram Type Descriptions", *Enneagram Institute*. Retrieved 12.7.19 from https://www.enneagraminstitute.com/type-descriptions.

Now, as clearly as I see that defining moment in time of learning my father had Parkinson's Disease, I can feel my heart sink when thinking of how our lives will be forever changed. I remember exactly how my Dad responded to that turning point in his life. Parkinson's may be the worst thing that will ever happen to my father, but Greg Ritscher may be the best thing that has happened to Parkinson's Disease. He immediately sought out studies to be a part of. He got in the best shape of his life to keep the symptoms as distant of a reality as he could. There were the support groups, boxing club, and speaking gigs he began participating in.

The strangest thing started to happen. My father, the self-proclaimed "Warlord of Commerce", a businessman who I had only seen cry two times in my 25 years of existence, was becoming the father I always needed. Now please don't get me wrong; Greg Ritscher was one of the most incredible dads the world has ever known. He was always strong, smart, provided for my every need, and knew the Lord and His Word so deeply, but let's just say that he wasn't known for his tenderness. The vulnerability that comes with Parkinson's absolutely has been a blessing in disguise for my life. Love sometimes can be a better tool versus logic when parenting.

I've come to understand one major fact of life through this experience. The world will always tell you to not let certain situations define you, to shrug it off, and move forward. What I've come to realize though is that it can be very important to let something define you, to take something on wholeheartedly, both the good and the bad of it. What you CAN choose is the impact that such definition will have in your life and the lives of others. The life of my family will always be defined not by Parkinson's Disease, but how we responded to it. After all, this may be the greatest part of our journey together.

To one he gave five bags of gold, to another two bags, and to another one bag, each according to his ability. Then he went on his journey. The man who had received five bags of gold went at once and put his money to work and gained five bags more. So also, the one with two bags of gold gained two more. But the man who had received one bag went off, dug a hole in the ground, and hid his master's money.

After a long time the master of those servants returned and settled accounts with them. The man who had received five bags of gold brought the other five. 'Master,' he said, 'you entrusted me with five bags of gold. See, I have gained five more.'

His master replied, 'Well done, good and faithful servant! You have been faithful with a few things; I will put you in charge of many things. Come and share your master's happiness!'

The man with two bags of gold also came. 'Master,' he said, 'you entrusted me with two bags of gold; see, I have gained two more.'

His master replied, 'Well done, good and faithful servant! You have been faithful with a few things; I will put you in charge of many things. Come and share your master's happiness!'

Then the man who had received one bag of gold came. 'Master,' he said, 'I knew that you are a hard man, harvesting where you have not sown and gathering where you have not scattered seed. So I was afraid and went out and hid your gold in the ground. See, here is what belongs to you.'

'His master replied, 'You wicked, lazy servant! So you knew that I harvest where I have not sown and gather where I have not scattered seed? Well then, you should have put my money on deposit with the bankers, so that when I returned I would have received it back with interest. So take the bag of gold from him and give it to the one who has ten bags. For whoever has will be given more, and they will have an abundance. Whoever does not have, even what they have will be taken from them. And throw that worthless servant outside, into the darkness, where there will be weeping and gnashing of teeth.'

Matthew 25:15-30

CHAPTER 8

REDEFINING BIG PROBLEMS

BREAKING UP BIG PROBLEMS
INTO SMALLER ONES

At this point in the book, I don't want you to think life is rosy. Who am I kidding? Parkinson's impact on my life extends into every role I assume and tasks I've tried to accomplish. Talk about reach and endurance – PD has a very tight hold on my life! The real trouble with Parkinson's Disease is that so many of the worst symptoms are non-motor in nature. It is bad enough to have tremors and muscle stiffness every waking moment, but the most debilitating symptoms are often hidden from society.

One of the many critical, negative traits of Parkinson's, which goes unseen is the quickness with which depression or anxiety floods over your thinking. You can be having a perfectly happy day, then suddenly you think everything is a mess and it is all your fault.

The largest number of Parkinson's Disease symptoms have to do with fatigue. PD attacks the portion of your brain that controls sound sleep. Additionally, Parkinson's attacks the portion of your brain that stops you from physically acting out your dreams. Many nights I wake up swinging my arms wildly to beat up a figment of my dreams. My wife and I are forced to sleep with a pillow separating us for her protection.

Night terrors are another example of Parkinson's ability to ruin your sleep. Take your worst nightmare, cube it, put it in living color, and you have a glimpse of what I deal with. Often, I will wake up from hitting my hand on the bed or falling out of bed. I'll be so charged up about my vivid dream that I will not go back to sleep, just so I do not have to finish the dream!

All these symptoms which cause poor sleeping habits, lead to a trait called REM (Rapid Eye Movement) Deprivation. Your body does not get to stay in REM sleep long enough for your mind to download today's events into your short-term memory. This overloads your brain's ability to clear the RAM (Random Access Memory) portion of your brain. This is like having a messy desk all the time. You cannot get anything done because you cannot find anything.

Micrographia is another persistent result of Parkinson's. Imagine how many words you hand write in a day and how important those words are. Now, start writing a note with your normal size writing and with each successive word make it 10% smaller. No wonder I cannot read my own notes 20 minutes later!

Throw in drooling, choking on food, a dead-pan look on your face, a diminished ability to regulate your body temperature, and you can see why Parkinson's — though not instantly fatal — is very difficult to live with.

Did I mention constant constipation? I will not even go there! This Parkinson's event is a huge problem for me to deal with for the rest of my life. I often ask myself, "What could I have accomplished — both in business and personally — if I didn't have to expend so much energy fighting off the negative effects of PD?" I repeatedly turn to a tried and true model that I call the "Big Problem Square".

MODEL:
SOLVE BIG PROBLEMS

Atomic Events, by their very nature, are BIG PROBLEMS. Often BIG PROBLEMS appear unsolvable, based on our past experiences, which creates F.E.A.R. in our minds and leads us into the "Dead Zone" of thinking about crisis and change. If we go back to the previous chapter, this creates Level Four Uncertainty — the highest level — which leads us to think that our future outcomes are both unknown and unknowable. Using the Adversity Quotient formula, it is apparent that we need to increase our self-awareness and self-management skill sets to do this. Let's take a look at the BIG PROBLEMS model, then relate it to dealing with Parkinson's.

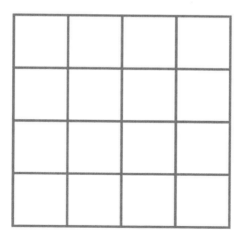

In the image above, how many squares do you see? Now show the image to a few other people — maybe even members of your support team — and ask them the same question. Answers generally start at 16; some might say 17; occasionally you might even hear 21. Rarely you will hear 26, but the actual answer is that there are 30 squares in this grid.

How are there 30 distinct squares in this graphic? The answer to this problem, just like the BIG PROBLEM in your life, is more easily seen if you take the big figure and break it down into its components. To answer the question correctly, "How many squares do you see?", you first need to remember the definition of a square: a plane figure with four equal straight sides and four right angles. Now do you see them, all of them?

Learning to visualize what each of the different types of squares consists of (One-by-One, Two-by-Two, etc.) is just like dealing with my Parkinson's Disease diagnosis one square at a time. The first thing I did was to learn everything I could about the disease. I read books from various support groups, associations, and medical journals. I needed to vastly increase my intellectual understanding of the physiological structure of the brain, how it functions, and what goes wrong when you have Parkinson's. I learned all about the basal ganglia, substantia nigra, Lewy bodies, dopamine, alpha-synuclein proteins, and genetic predisposition. I learned as much as I could about what is connected to what, and how it all works together. I also discovered as much as I could about how PD causes my physiology to change or malfunction.

Let's go back to the squares model. The easiest way to count the number of squares is to start by counting the squares one-by-one. Counting four rows of four squares each gives us the first part of the answer: 4 x 4 = 16. Most people see this easily. But to solve the problem completely, we need to look deeper for additional hidden relationships between elements to find more sets of squares.

Generally, the next additional square that people see is the Four-by-Four square or the big picture border of the whole graphic model. We live in a big picture culture where we are not so worried about the details as we are about the end results. It is easy for people to stop here by counting the Four-by-Four and One-by-One squares. But we need to keep looking because there are more squares to count.

If there are One-by-One and Four-by-Four squares, shouldn't there be Two-by-Two squares? Look closely at the figure to see more than just the obvious answer. Two, One-by-One squares stacked on top of each other and two next to each other create a square that is two-lines long by two-lines wide. At first glance, it just looks like there are four different Two-by-Two squares, but remember we need to look more closely at the graphic to see that there are actually three distinct Two-by-Two squares in each row. Each of these Two-by-Two squares has a distinct column of One-by-One boxes and a shared column of One-by-One boxes. There are three distinct boxes in each column, which make nine distinct Two-by-Two squares in this model.

Last but not least, people rarely think of the Three-by-Three squares that exist in each of the four corners of the figure. Now that I've mentioned it, can you see them? These are the last critical components to coming up with the correct total answer of 30 squares.

Now, let's relate this to Parkinson's Disease. Use this grid to break down the BIG PROBLEM of PD by naming the 16 largest components that are impacting your life. I labeled each corner of the whole grid with Cognitive, Motor, Non-Motor, and Psychological symptoms. Then, I filled in the four worst problems that I deal with in each of those areas. You can check out my BIG PROBLEM grid on the next page.

The Four-by-Four Square is the reality of the Atomic Event. In its entirety, it is overwhelming. I do not walk around with a sign that says, "I have Parkinson's", but I do notice people reacting to my symptoms, particularly my tremors. Having PD changes not only everything in my life, but also how people view me. The Two-by-Two squares are the unique combination of effects of the individual symptoms being grouped together. As an example, the One-by-One squares of poor sleep, deadpan face, quiet voice, and zoning out are often negatively interpreted by others that I am anti-social or don't care about them. Nothing could be further from the truth.

MOTOR					NON-MOTOR
	TREMOR	QUIET VOICE	CONSTI-PATION	POOR SLEEP	
	POOR BALANCE	DROOL	NIGHT TERRORS	FATIGUE	
	FRUSTRA-TION	FORGET FULNESS	GLOOMY OUTLOOK	DEADPAN FACE	
	LOSS OF JOB	LACK OF COGNITION	ZONING OUT	OVERLY EMOTIONAL	
COGNITIVE					PSYCHO-LOGICAL

Your Parkinson's or other Atomic Event may have different cornerstone effects. I always look at my own model once a year to stay in touch with any changing issues that might have popped up in my life.

The Three-by-Three squares are the hardest to see side-effects of Parkinson's in my life. If I — or someone close to me — observes and mentions a behavior change to me, I can learn to look for the second or third answer. For example, poor sleep, anxiety, and tremors all create a bad atmosphere for public speaking. These can lead to an appearance of nervousness, and as a result, people stop listening to what I am saying and simply watch my symptoms.

The BIG PROBLEM — aka your Atomic Event — can thus be broken down from Four-by-Four views into smaller problems, which are more easily dealt with. But you must take a long-term view of your symptoms morphing over time, one day at a time, by always keeping an open mind and being willing to take an honest look at all the things you are dealing with.

A surprising thing I have learned after looking at the Three-by-Three and Two-by-Two squares of the BIG PROBLEM of PD, is that I will reach far more people and have a bigger influence in their lives BECAUSE I have PD, not IN SPITE OF having PD. Breaking down the BIG PROBLEM of Parkinson's into smaller, easier to see components has allowed me to share insights through poetry, speaking to support groups, participating in research studies, and even writing this book. My support team people say that I am now much kinder and gentler towards others, a better listener, and a far more influential person in their lives. In my poem (Chapter One) the line "disease ambassador unleashed" refers to this expanding circle of influence. Hopefully, my life is an example to others that you truly can harness the negative energy of an Atomic Event and turn it into a positive life force for others.

RISE POINT:
PARKINSON'S AS THE BIG PROBLEM

Every major problem you face can be broken down into sub-components, some of which you may have a solution for. Thus, you can start to fill in the squares and reduce some uncertainty in your decisions to solve the original BIG PROBLEM. There are many symptoms for every person with Parkinson's. So, first try to solve the smaller squares that you can; this will give you better guidance for solving the BIG PROBLEM.

VANTAGE POINT:

NATHAN HEIMER,
SON-IN-LAW

I vividly remember getting a phone call from Mindy (my wife) and hearing her tell me through tears that her dad was diagnosed with Parkinson's Disease. I was absolutely speechless and instantly overwhelmed with a sense of grief. My mind began to race with questions. "What does this mean?" "What will the future look like?" "How fast will it progress?" "Why him?" Many of these questions I'm sure will never have a definitive answer, but they were there, and they were real. Reality for Greg and those around him changed instantly — and in that moment — it was okay to have more questions than answers. It was almost impossible at that time to see the bigger picture.

My focus narrowed in on the diagnosis and sadness for the journey that awaited my father-in-law. In the minutes — then hours — following that call, the grief seemed to intensify. Even more questions came flooding in and more emotions seemed to surface ... anger, frustration, and hopelessness. It was incredibly hard to view, let alone understand, the road forward.

Later that night, Mindy, Haven (our son), and I went over to my in-laws' home. Seeing Greg in person brought an instant sense of relief. The same man that we knew and loved was still there. Often, our human nature tends to immediately think of the worst possible scenario. It isn't until we see and talk to the person that we gain perspective. He was alive, he was strong (still way stronger than me!), and though the road forward had now taken a different direction, he was and is still Greg.

I know that this diagnosis has shaken Greg to his core, yet he has never backed down. He has risen to the occasion to not only battle this for himself, but he has taken up the fight for the many others affected by Parkinson's Disease. I have heard him say often that he would do anything to make sure his grandkids would never have to experience this. It seemed like almost immediately following the diagnosis, Greg was signing up for studies, taking part in support groups, speaking, and sharing his story. He was doing whatever he could to shine a light on and create a way forward for those dealing with Parkinson's. Along with this, Greg continued to share the importance of his faith through his words and actions. His faith in God is unwavering and absolutely instrumental in his journey with Parkinson's.

Over the years, his symptoms have negatively progressed. His tremors are more noticeable, he tires more quickly, but he is still a force to be reckoned with. Greg is still incredibly active: he does boxing, hiking, paddle boarding, running, and yoga. Best of all, Greg does almost anything his grandsons ask of him. His activity level has had a major effect on slowing the progression of his symptoms. I'm not kidding when I say that he is still in better shape and stronger than I am!

I am beyond blessed to have Greg as a father-in-law. He is an inspiration to me and I am constantly amazed at the way he has responded to his PD diagnosis thus far. I know that this journey has not been easy, but I love the way he continues to live and fight. I can honestly say that someday I hope and pray to be half the man that Greg is.

"The Lord will fight for you; you need only to be still."
Exodus 14:14

CHAPTER 9

EMBRACING CHANGE

THE ROLE OF CHANGE
IN CREATING PROGRESS

"The only constant is change."[21] That's a common saying in leadership circles. It becomes cliche, but it helps leaders chart the course for the future path they will take in life. "So, how am I going to deal with this sudden change to my life?" is a common thought of mine. I know that everyone is watching my reaction to my diagnosis — my wife, daughters, family, friends, and fellow teammates at work. Here is a perfect chance to implement what I have learned about life changes and how to quickly adapt to them.

When we face unexpected changes, having a long-term vision in place will help us know how to navigate the change, yet still stay on our life's course. This is where my "Vision Statement" came in. I needed to continue striving to live up to my life's vision statement:

[21] Tendeiro, Jorge. "Heraclitus: The Only Constant is Change". *Socratic Life*. 10.16.17. Retrieved 3.24.2020 from https://socraticlife.com.au/heraclitus-the-only-constant-is-change/.

Using the talents God has given me to their fullest, in a loving manner,
I will have a positive impact on everyone's life that I touch.
I want to be known as a "Visionary Maven," a person who
helps others achieve more than they thought
they could achieve in their own lives.

My vision statement helped me get back on course for my life when Parkinson's side-swiped me, bringing unwanted changes. Because I already had a vision statement for my life, I knew the correct course I had to get back on, and keep moving forward as I navigated the roadblocks and reroutes of PD.

Another mentor in my life, Duane Keesen, taught me a thing or two about understanding change in every aspect of my life. Duane is older than I, so he is in a life phase in front of me. He is a man of God, and has thrived in his life despite a number of Atomic Events trying to derail him.

He has all the great attributes to look for in a mentor:

- We share the same values and beliefs: faith, family, and integrity in both our personal and business dealings.

- He is one life phase ahead of me. Duane has been retired for a number of years and has already gone through that stage of learning to redirect his energies toward the common good of people. I just retired in January of 2019 and am learning from him how to refocus my efforts in a similar manner.

- His tenacity is to be admired. He "cowboys up" in every phase of his life.

Duane and I have met monthly for 20-some years. He has been the most influential man in my adult life, and I can never repay him. So I am "paying it forward" by using the skills he taught me to younger men whom I now mentor.

For example, Duane is very active in his home church and volunteers to do all kinds of things. He is a behind-the-scenes type of person and tries to stay out of the limelight. He has helped a number of my friends out of tough situations by using his experience. He is the most humble man I know. I need to learn to behave this way!

Duane has also taught me how to be a better parent to adult children. How to help them deal with divorce, career changes, and financial distress are all examples of things I have learned from him.

Maybe Duane's best lesson for me has come in the area of learning to be more empathetic and wise. Tapping into his "tree of knowledge" and understanding his style of wisdom have both made me a better person.

A mentor like Duane is an experienced and trusted advisor. I have always looked for mentors at every stage of my life. Why not learn from people who have experienced similar situations that you find yourself in? Sometimes you learn what to do and sometimes you learn what not to do. F.A.I.L. is an acronym for the phrase "First Attempt In Learning". That is exactly what dealing with Atomic Events in your life is about. No one knows how they will react in a crisis change, like the death of a spouse or child, until they actually experience it. The good news is that once you handle a traumatic event, and live through it, you now have the "gift" of experience and empathy to give someone going through a similar event.

As a participant in the Leeds School of Business Professional Mentoring Program at the University of Colorado, one group of students I have mentored are collegiate juniors. I am matched with a junior and stay with them for two years through their graduation. During our monthly meetings and phone conversations, I try to impart knowledge and wisdom to my mentee about majors to choose from, classes to take, interviewing skills, and networking to obtain internships and job placement. But the most important thing I do is to teach them 'bounce-back skills' for when changes occur in their lives.

One of my mentees came from a family with a long line of accountants who were all part of a family business. He was an accounting major, but I could see that accounting was not in his heart. Instead, working with junior high school youth was. I arranged for him to have dinner with several professional youth workers so he could hear all the angles of youth ministry. He decided to pursue ministry as a profession. We practiced interviewing skills and he was able to land a job working with junior high youth in Colorado. Facilitating change in a person's life can be tricky, but the more you know about change, the easier it is to manage it.

MODEL:
THREE FORMS OF CHANGE

What is "changing" about change? It is happening at a faster pace and in more radical and discontinuous ways than ever before. You used to have a good 10-15 minutes to prepare your business or family to respond to an Atomic Event that just occurred. Today, with smartphones, camera drones, and social media you have perhaps 30 seconds to develop a response to calm the "media" of your life. Live video technology apps like Facetime, Skype, Zoom, and psychographic generational influences, all make for immediate intrusion into your life. These further speed up the pace of change and the scope of how it influences your life.

Today, change does not follow any type of pattern. When I was young, the bad guys figured out how to hijack airplanes to get the world's attention for some political cause. Just think of how air travel has changed in the last twenty years! After 9/11, planes are not just modes of travel but are now weapons of mass destruction. And, media centers via smartphones show the world what is going on right now in even the most remote nations.

Even things like values and beliefs, which are not supposed to change with time, are being impacted at a faster pace. LOVE is a value, and at one point in your life — if you are lucky enough to be married — you promised to love your spouse, "Till death do us part." Honestly, do you love your spouse the same way and with the same intensity today as you did on your wedding day?

My personal experience with LOVE as a value — after forty years of marriage — is quite broad. My wife and I have survived numerous Atomic Events including daughters with dating issues, psychological disorders, athletic injuries requiring surgery, parents passing away, and the death of close friends. All of these rocked our world in an instant. However, my love has both grown abundantly (I love her for more reasons) and strengthened deeper (more Agape-type love) not in spite of these events, but because of them.

Yet, research statistics tell us that for more than half the people who marry, their marriage will somehow change to a point where they agree to go their separate ways. Dealing with the symptoms of Parkinson's WILL put a lot of pressure on any relationship, and the speed with which these symptoms arise is incredibly quick. That will heap serious stress on any marriage!

Beliefs, which are supposed to be far more lasting than Values, are even changing at a faster pace. In my world, my beliefs about the medicinal value of marijuana — and the acceptance of CBD's — has changed with the advent of new information, which science has made us aware of.

Parkinson's Disease is like this. Some symptoms come and go as they please (night terrors, constipation) while other symptoms change in severity on a daily basis (tremors, fatigue). In Parkinson's lingo we call it being "On" or "Off". It seems that PD has a mind of its own. You can regulate when you take your medicines, or what you consume in your diet, but Parkinson's is always wreaking havoc with your body's biorhythms.

The great mystery about change is that we both resist and seek it, simultaneously. Think about relationships and changes for single people considering marriage. If change is seen as possibly creating a better environment, a smoothing out of life for the better, or helping make sense of the future (giving hope), then a single person seeks out change and gets married. On the other hand, if they perceive change as possibly generating a worse environment, a loss of the normal flow in their life, or perhaps the illusion of a foreboding future, then they will resist the change and remain single.

Humans resist change for two powerful reasons:

1. **Homeostasis** – We seek a condition of balance or equilibrium through self-regulation. Examples are: how your body regulates its temperature or your blood sugar levels. This is the desire to adhere to the saying "The more things change, the more they stay the same."

    Bill Murray's movie, *Groundhog Day*, was about a character who kept living the same day over and over again. At first, he liked it because it helped him "predict" the future and he became a local hero. Eventually, he got stuck in a rut and wanted to change and move on.

2. **Loss** – All change involves giving something up. If we fear loss more than the unpleasantness of our current circumstances, then we will resist change. Consider people who remain in a dead-end job or who stay with an abusive spouse.

    Daryl Conner in his book, *Managing at the Speed of Change*,[22] states, "Pain or loss must be a forecaster of possibility. We must learn to orchestrate pain/loss factors to be successful in handling change in our lives."

Both homeostasis and loss do not distinguish between "good" or "bad" change; they just cause us to resist all change.

---

[22] Conner, Daryl R. *Managing at the Speed of Change: How Resilient Managers Succeed and Prosper Where Others Fail*. 1993. Random House. New York, NY.

Change also weakens our bonds to an organization, person, or cause. That is why you must work at staying in love with the people you have made a commitment to love forever. Change such as being diagnosed with Parkinson's Disease makes us feel helpless, powerless, and vulnerable. These are the components that lead to a victim mindset. Despite your best efforts to stay positive, it's easy to dislike all this change as it is being heaped onto you. Hence, with the fear that comes from uncertainty, the weakening of bonds to those we love, and the victim mentality, is it any wonder that in a company undergoing lots of change, some people quit and leave, while others threaten to quit and instead stay? The latter is far more threatening to an organization!

On the other side of the coin, we do seek change for several reasons.

1. **Purpose** – Change can give us a greater sense of purpose in our lives. Think of how the effect of having children influences people. It either gives them a much greater sense of purpose (family unity/ bonding), so they are willing to put up with the turmoil of child-rearing — or for some — it drives them away because it is too much responsibility, and that is not the purpose they saw in their lives. The key to managing change is PURPOSE.

2. **Fulfillment** – You can choose to do whatever you like, as long as you are willing to pay the price. You do not have a choice on facing change in your life, but you clearly control how you will react to it. Is there any greater sense of worth than when you realize you have faced a major change required in your life, and you have orchestrated a harmonious transition?

    This is the golden answer in our lives. It is the sense of accomplishment you feel when you know you have given it your all, and you have become better for it. Returning to a high level of fitness — through a well-planned work out regimen — to help you with many of Parkinson's motor and non-motor symptoms, is a classic example.

Change tends to come in three different forms:

1. **Crisis Change** – This is change abruptly thrust upon you, like hearing, "You've got Parkinson's Disease", the merger of two businesses being suddenly announced, or a tragedy involving a loved one. It happens suddenly! You usually blame it on factors beyond your control, everyone around you senses it, and people are "sensitive" to your recovery from it. Crisis change creates the quickest response; everyone loves to pitch in and help.

2. **Evolutionary Change** (or "better late than never" change) – If you wait long enough, maybe things will go back to the way they were. This change happens slowly. Everyone looks to blame the change on someone else; not all of the people involved see the change occurring; and people have differing levels of sensitivity to your recovery. Some people who still do not see the change wonder why you are different, while others wonder what took you so long to do something about it. Evolutionary change causes the most turmoil in our lives, because we do not see it coming. That is why I do a yearly assessment of my Parkinson's, which involves about 20 different factors to compare slow moving, evolutionary changes with the previous year. I also send out an email to my family and support group on the anniversary of my diagnosis and ask them if they have noticed any changes over the last year and what those are.

3. **Visionary Change** – This change is proactive and empowering. It comes from anticipating, creating, and learning. If handled correctly, it offers first-strike advantage to the visionary. Although if it happens too quickly and no one else "sees" the change, it generates the most resistance. If no one else sees the change like you do, they will all question the change and your loyalty to them.

    Often, it is difficult to explain visionary change as it may be just a hunch or a feeling. It certainly generates lots of questions. But if you can answer the questions and show congruence with the vision of the team, it provides you with the strongest sense of bonding and strength to accomplish the task. Faith is a stronghold of vision, because it gives you a guideline to follow in the form of commands, precepts, and statutes (Psalm 19: 7-9). The Bible uses two imperatives (a command sentence where the unwritten subject is "you"), *Do not fear ...* and, *Fear not ...* over 300 times with quick explanations — which are God's precepts or statutes — immediately following each.

Therefore, visionary change for the righteous requires faith without fear based on the Word of God.

Often, one type of change leads to another type of change. For example, the destruction of a hurricane (crisis) often leads to a better and smarter rebuilding of the destroyed area (visionary). Likewise, a forest fire (crisis) can burn down a mature forest which supports very little life, but opens up the canopy in the trees — allowing sunlight to hit the forest floor and re-grow the entire ecosystem — which supports abundant life forms (evolutionary). Of course it is very difficult living through the crisis of the hurricane or fire and the aftermath.

Parkinson's Disease is no different. The initial diagnosis is crisis change, but if you stay on top of the evolutionary change that occurs, and even introduce some visionary change (i.e. boxing, hiking up 14,000' mountains), you can often mitigate or at least delay some of the worst effects.

Change as a process has three distinct stages. The more you know about the stages of change, the easier it is to move through them. They are:

1. **Letting Go** — When resistance is at its peak, friends and family cannot see what the visionary person can, thus they question the visionary's motives. They may even sabotage the fledgling efforts of the visionary as they attempt to implement the change. Different groups of people will break off based on what they see in the change. Early adopters (10%) will want to move with the visionary out of loyalty, even if they

don't really see the need for the change. Laggards (20%), the last of the group to see the change, are dead set on dragging their feet because they are comfortable with the status quo.

The key group to influence is the median masses (70%). They can sense that something needs to change, but they just can't see a good reason to cross the street. They were willing to go halfway across the street, because they saw the early adopters do it. But now with car traffic on both sides of them, they think it is safer to stay on the median and let some more time go by. These people will experience a whole range of emotions including anger, blame, denial, and despair.

In the world of Parkinson's, once you have heard your diagnosis and accept that you have the disease, early adopters will be doing anything to hold off the disease, i.e.: research studies and joining support groups. The median masses will join in or start some type of response, but they will not follow through. They will stall until the pain of doing nothing moves them out of the median and heading for some type of constructive change. The laggards remain dead set against any change and are soon just dead.

2. **Dead Zone** – This is the time when you feel the worst. You no longer have what you once had, yet you do not know what the future holds for you. F.E.A.R (Future Expectations Appear Real) takes over — the human mind always focuses on the worst things that can happen to you rather than the best things happening to you — because that is instinctually how our early ancestors stayed alive. You tend to feel both confusion and adjustment; there is both despair and hope. Kanter's Law states, "Every change looks like a failure in the middle".[23] That is why it is imperative to get the median masses to see the change and finish crossing the street. In the Parkinson's world, this is usually the zone you fall into when you are first diagnosed. There is despair because now you know you have a life-threatening disease. There is also a glimmer of hope because maybe you know someone who has learned to thrive as they live with the disease.

---

[23] Kanter, Rosabeth Moss. "Change is Hardest in the Middle". *HBR*. 8.12.2009. Retreived 3.14.2020 from https://hbr.org/2009/08/change-is-hardest-in-the-middl.

3. **The Leap** – This happens when the 51st percentile of your group begins to see the new way. They will feel both fear and excitement as they let go of the old way to embrace the new reality. You start to introduce the change as "the way" of moving forward towards a better future by using creativity and imagination. The truth is "you see it, when you believe it", but you can only see it after you change your paradigm. Not the other way around.

There are many aspects to dealing with change in our lives, not the least of which is just taking the necessary time to learn about it. Like any skill, if you learn the basics, practice regularly, and have the aptitude to want to do well, you can develop the habit of successfully dealing with any Atomic Event in your life whether it is Parkinson's or some other type of crisis. This is one of the most critical life skills you can learn.

RISE POINT:
MOVE BEYOND SURVIVING A CRISIS

Now, let's relate this to dealing with Parkinson's in your own life and the changes that follow. Remember when I said humans resist change for two important reasons? Well, PD is really a double whammy in the arena of change. First, Parkinson's severely disrupts our state of homeostasis: it throws us off balance and changes almost every aspect of our day-to-day lives. Second, Parkinson's entails a large amount of loss: we lose many functions and abilities that we relied on for most of our lives. Parkinson's starts out as a Crisis change with the initial diagnosis and all the fears and unknowns that go with the initial shock. Then as you settle into your new normal, PD turns into Evolutionary change with its many fine features and slow progressions. You can easily get stuck in either of these first two stages of change depending on your ability to resolve the many issues associated with each. Personally, I choose to live in stage three, Visionary change. My internal locus of control allowed me to quickly accept both the PURPOSE and FULFILLMENT of why I have Parkinson's in my life. I can now see how Parkinson's helps fulfill the Vision Statement for my life: it frees me to take the leap and live a life wherein I am THRIVING with Parkinson's. Take that PD!

VANTAGE POINT:

DUANE KEESEN,
PERSONAL MENTOR

From both a business and personal perspective, I have known Greg for about 30 years. I have been a mentor to Greg for over 20 years. I agreed to mentor Greg only because of all the mistakes or events in my life that — by the grace of God — I have learned from. Having run the race for 75 years, I strongly believe that my purpose in life is not yet complete.

I have known Greg both before and after his Parkinson's diagnosis, which included his battle with Prostate Cancer. One of the traits that helps Greg deal with Atomic Events in his life is that he does not see himself as the center of his life; his family and others are the center of his focus.

Greg is highly intellectual. He likes to create an atmosphere which enables people to live better, fuller lives. He believes that developing people is one of the gifts God has given him. He knows the importance of leading by example and applies this to his daily activities.

Greg is very competitive and has always enjoyed playing team sports. He started to realize something was wrong with his physical health while playing basketball. Greg noticed he could not control the ball with his right hand and would occasionally miss a step. His team sport competitive spirit now helps him tremendously by battling Parkinson's with everything he has. He is in great physical shape, using exercise boot camp and yoga to stay balanced and social.

Greg lives a purpose-filled life. He looks in a positive light at all he can learn from the experiences God allows him to go through, both good and bad. With God's help, he is not afraid to confront and face a challenging issue. Sharing these experiences with others makes him a very effective motivational person.

One of the hardest things in my life is asking for help from other people. It is especially hard to ask those you love the most — your wife and family. I have found joy and satisfaction when I help others. When I do not allow others to help me, I am robbing them of that same joy! This is a lesson I am trying to teach Greg now. God had a purpose when he introduced me to Greg, for both of us!

The law of the Lord is perfect, refreshing the soul. The statutes of the Lord are trustworthy, making wise the simple. The precepts of the Lord are right, giving joy to the heart. The commands of the Lord are radiant, giving light to the eyes. The fear of the Lord is pure, enduring forever. The decrees of the Lord are firm, and all of them are righteous.
Psalm 19:7-9

CHAPTER 10

INTERNAL LOCUS OF CONTROL

YOU ALWAYS HAVE
CHOICES IN ANY SITUATION

It took me some time to rebound from the initial shock of hearing I had Parkinson's Disease. Over time, I realized I needed to build a survival plan. In the universe there are three things I know I cannot stop: black holes from growing; the passage of time's effects on my aging body; and the negative effects of Parkinson's worsening over time. There is no sense in wishing it would go away (it will not). There is no sense in giving up and just letting Parkinson's proceed to destroy my life. Like Steve Wurst shared back in *Chapter 5*, "In your life, if you find yourself in a hole, the first thing to do is stop digging." Even if the Atomic Event is not your fault (remember C.O.O.R.E.), you still need to focus on what you can do to improve the situation.

The only actual difference between "OPPORTUNITY IS NOWHERE" and "OPPORTUNITY IS NOW HERE", is where you put an extra space! It is up to you to put the emphasis in the spot you want. When life deals you an Atomic Event, be prepared, think ahead, and have the framework put in place to deal with the issue.

I found that placing borders, also known as "margins",[24] to stay inside the lines of a reasonable life helped me create order and let my mind catch up to everything that was happening. Exercise is one way I do this on a nearly daily basis. Not only does working out release neurochemicals which improve my outlook, it also gives me a sense of accomplishment, helps with my balance and coordination. Most importantly, I have developed a sense of community at my gym, which has been especially important to me and my family.

Boxing and yoga are two activities that I pursue in fighting off the effects of Parkinson's. I practiced yoga prior to my diagnosis, but I mainly did it to stay limber to prolong my athletic career. After my PD diagnosis, I started to practice yoga in earnest because it is so helpful in re-teaching me balance. Yoga also helps me stay socialized as I often see the same people in my 6 am yoga class. Mastering a certain pose and learning new ones all the time also releases lots of neurochemicals into my brain. Therefore, I feel the best I will feel all day after a yoga class.

I do not know what affects people with Parkinson's more than a good, one-hour boxing lesson. There is something triggered in a Parkinson's brain which helps to broaden people's talents and beliefs in themselves. I often watch my fellow Parkie's come into our boxing class on Saturday mornings and observe they are hunched over and shuffling. Within ten minutes of starting our boxing drills, these same people are moving around much better, standing up straight — and more importantly — laughing and having a good time.

---

[24] Swensen, Richard. *Margin: Restoring Emotional, Physical, Financial, and Time Reserves to Overloaded Lives*. 2004. NavPress. Colorado Springs, CO.

Have you ever noticed how when things go wrong in your life it seems like everything runs together? Trouble seems to come in twos and threes. The pressure of having to deal with an emergency keeps your focus so tied up, you do not notice the passage of time. Thus when bad event #2 comes along, your perception is that it was tied to bad event #1. Without the proper margin in your life, you do not get to have a breather to stay focused on developing and implementing the right course of action after the first bad event.

A perfect example of this in most people's lives would be estate planning. Statistics tell us the older we get, the chances of us passing away greatly increase. Yet many people do not have a will or other estate planning completed, and if by chance they would pass away, they leave a mess for their spouse or heirs to deal with. It is called the tyranny of the urgent versus the important.

We live such fast-paced lives (no margin), we do not take the time on our own — or meet with professionals to help us — to draw up a Last Will and Testament or have a financial plan in place to express our wishes for the disbursement of our estate. I knew a young married couple that had the world by the tail. Both had great jobs, they shared a beautiful home, and enjoyed several nice assets. The husband of this pair had emigrated from China as a child and had no living relatives in the US. They did not have a will or any estate plan.

When he died suddenly, his entire estate was left to his parents — who live in China — because with no will, his assets and life insurance benefits from his employment went to his parents whom he had listed as beneficiaries years earlier. Unfortunately, he had not remembered to switch his named beneficiary on his policy to his wife because he was a very busy person building his empire. No margin in his life led to immense grief for his young widow. She was left dealing with all the burial issues while his assets were held up in court. All of his insurance money and assets — which she badly needed and could have used if available to her through his will — were sent to his parents based on state probate laws.

Those of us with Parkinson's Disease know how learning to deal with the symptoms takes away from some parts of the margin of our lives. What we need to learn is that PD can actually help build margin into our life. Parkinson's forced me to retire earlier than I had planned, but it also now gives me added time to focus on the really important life goals I want to achieve. My life is now far more focused on being significant in other people's lives and not so focused on my own personal successes. Being more on purpose with my life, I hope to live a richer life in the time I have remaining.

MODEL:
INTERNAL VS. EXTERNAL LOCUS OF CONTROL

In 1954, a psychologist by the name of Julian Rotter,[25] developed a component of personality psychology called Locus of Control. Locus stands for describing a stance or place. Locus is a point which varies its position according to influences exerted upon it. Control relates to the degree that a person prescribes to any phenomenon, which they think has direct causation in determining a present condition. Thus Locus of Control describes the extent to which an individual believes they can control events affecting them currently. How much power does one have over the events which occur in their life? People are measured on a scale based on the following factors:

- Awareness you have a choice in the situation
- Capability to review all options
- Capacity to remember your choices for future decisions
- Determination to choose what is best for you
- Willingness to ask for ideas

---

[25] "Locus of Control". *Changing Minds*. Retrieved 2.9.2020 from http://changingminds.org/explanations/preferences/locus_control.htm

There are two major types of Locus of Control:

1. **Internal Locus of Control** describes people who believe they have an impact on anything that happens to them. "I can control how I handle what happens to me in a given time frame." Internal Locus of Control people are often motivated to achieve some key factor in their lives — despite the present circumstances — to reach a particular outcome.

2. **External Locus of Control** describes people who regard efforts to alter a predetermined event as wasteful, so instead they focus on living with whatever happens to them with little to no effort expended for controlling the situation.

People can move back and forth between these two phases of Locus of Control, based on their current state of mind, energy levels, and past experiences. Knowledge of handling past issues and the inclination to look for new choices or alternative views of the future, also play a key role in determining your Locus of Control on any given issue.

I tend to have an Internal Locus of Control. I believe God has given me the talents and abilities to deal with virtually any issue life has thrown my way. By keeping a positive attitude, I believe that any event — good or bad — has a teaching component to it. It motivates me to find out what I need to learn from this event, then I can assimilate the scenario into a memory that is capable of helping others in the future. Proverbs 17:22 says, *A cheerful heart is good medicine, but a downcast spirit will dry out the bones.* You are either going to go through life laughing or crying. I choose to laugh.

Three Categories of Parkinson's Symptoms
I believe that an Internal Locus of Control will help virtually anyone deal with a diagnosis of Parkinson's Disease.

Let's look at the three major categories of Parkinson's symptoms: 1) Non-Motor, 2) Motor, and 3) Psychological. At first glance, each of these groups of symptoms appears to be a life-long anchor to drag around. But by using some of the components of Internal Locus of Control, we can quickly see that we do have a choice in how we respond to the situation. Remember, this is Victor Frankl's last, ultimate freedom: Response-Ability.

By using support groups and intellectually learning as much as you can about the physiology of these symptoms, you will be able to review your options, then choose a course of action that best fits your needs. As an example, I am determined to find "positive" aspects to having Parkinson's. So far, I have found three:

1. Non-Motor Symptoms – Loss of Smell. Positive: I can easily take out my grandson's dirty, smelly diapers to the trash.

2. Motor Symptoms – Tremor in right hand. Positive: I can better stir drinks and erase my grandson's writing on the wall.

3. Neurological Symptoms – Participate in research. Positive: I have honorarium money to put in my grandsons' 529 College Savings funds.

Dinner Plans
The following examples are shared with a touch of humor, but they do illustrate how we can look at challenges in a creative way.

Consider the major categories of Parkinson's symptoms as if we were out to eat dinner. Let's see if we can come up with a list of what we are up against as we strive to make menu choices for learning to thrive with this degenerate disease.

APPETIZERS – Non-Motor Symptoms
- Loss of Smell: Does not really impact life except for not being able to smell smoke or burning cookies.
- Lack of Matrix Thinking: Hard to remember variables to compare or judge. Did I turn on the stove?
- Constipation: Home remedies work (see *Endnotes C. page 183*). Need to watch diet and triggering foods (oatmeal, bananas).

- Cognition: Afternoon thinking slows; like thinking in mud; frozen words; frozen sentences.
- Loss of Confidence: Lack initiative; have apathy and asocial behavior; a feeling of checking out.
- Hypophonia: Quiet disposition and soft voice so others cannot hear; slurred speech.
- Poor Sleep Behavior: Have REM Deprivation; night terrors (the worst); impacts ability to drive alert.
- Hypo-Tension: Low blood pressure; have to be careful standing and turning simultaneously; take care to avoid falls.
- Dementia: As we live longer, this symptom increases; by 2035, 80% of people with Parkinson's will have some form of it.

Lack of smell is how I diagnosed myself. Constipation is a proverbial pain in the rear-end, but the lack of REM sleep leads to increasing difficulty with cognition and matrix thinking. Now think about what is on your table as an appetizer to the more physical symptoms.

MAIN COURSE – Motor Symptoms
- Tremor: Generally at rest; one side of the body: arms, legs and face. Stress increases tremors exponentially.
- Dyskinesia: Involuntary, jerky movement of hands, arm, shoulders. Tracks higher with increasing levels of dementia.
- Bradykinesia: Rigid muscles, stiffness in muscle group. Impacts even antagonistic muscle groups.
- Postural Instability: Lack of balance, slumped shoulders, shuffling feet, potential falls.
- Restless Leg: Keeps everyone awake, both partner and Parkie
- Hypokinesia: Abnormally diminished muscular mobility and function.
- Micrographic: Handwriting gets smaller and cramped. Writing in small, controlled movement.
- All autonomic nervous system functions including: Excessive drooling, perspiration, and GI tract issues.
- Dead arm swing: blank look on face, daytime sleepiness. These are all classic signs.

After seven years of battling tremors, now I am noticing an occasional episode of dyskinesia. Dementia cannot be far behind. I believe exercise is holding off the worst of the effects coming with the main course.

DESSERT – Neurological Symptoms
- Neurological: Hallucinations, illusions, and delirium.
- Paranoid Psychosis: Loss of intellectual abilities interfering with social functioning causing social withdrawal.
- Delusions: False, fixed beliefs. Cannot be persuaded against apparent alternative realities.
- Depression and Anxiety: Feeling of worry or borderline fear. All outcomes appear bleak.

With 'meals' like this to choose from, no wonder Parkinson's people don't like to go out! When I speak to groups, I often play the "Parkinson's Bingo Game." I made a card that shows the many different symptoms of Parkinson's. As we go through the description of each symptom, I hand out gift cards to the people who get a "Bingo" of symptoms.

Just as everyone's diagnosis of Parkinson's Disease is different, so is the set of symptoms each one of us experiences and deals with. For example, on my plate we start with some lack of smell, add in a heavy dose of constipation, top it off with poor sleep behavior, which leads to poor cognition and matrix thinking.

That's a lot to start a meal with if you also throw in a good-sized tremor, completely covered with autonomic nervous system dysfunctions, and put a micrography on top. Now, you have a big meal in-the-works!

Finish this all off with a heaping bowl of anxiety and you have a "meal deal" fit for a king. Add in the fact that PD is a degenerative, progressive disease, and things are getting shaking up in the food court of my life.

RISE POINT:
CHOOSE YOUR RESPONSE

By maintaining an Internal Locus of Control, I can choose my response to any stimuli Parkinson's or another Atomic Event sends my way (like Prostate Cancer in 2016). Exercise, yoga, and a "can do" attitude help me to put margin in my life. Focusing on the important things in life can both energize and prioritize your direction to determine where you are going and what you will do when you get there. Hopefully, like me, you will be able to see that despite having Parkinson's, OPPORTUNITY really is NOW HERE!

VANTAGE POINT:

MARTI SARTAIN,
LONG-TIME FRIEND

I have known Greg for about 25 years and we are good friends. I would do anything for him and he would do anything for me (within reason!). We have simply kept in touch over the years because of Greg. He has made a point to reach out to me and I followed suit. We text and talk on the phone a few times a year and manage to squeeze in a lunch at least once a year.

It is obvious to me that throughout his life, Greg has built, demonstrated, and honed-in on his life habits. He lives his life with purpose. Because of who he is and has become, I would expect nothing short of him being encouraged to write a book about his journey with Parkinson's Disease.

Once he discovered he had Parkinson's, he began educating himself about it, joined a support group, and was determined from the get-go to do everything he could to continue learning and doing his best to extend and live a quality life. Greg has always been very healthy and outgoing, playing basketball and other team or individual sports. I can't imagine what went through his mind when Greg learned he may not be able to do those things as well, as often, and probably not at all at some point in time.

But being the person Greg is, his reaction (after the shock) was to accept the prognosis, deciding he wasn't going to let PD destroy his life. He would do the best he could with the cards he was dealt. Another huge piece for Greg was to learn as much as he could about Parkinson's, so he could share what he's learned with others, helping them on their journeys. He has done this type of mentoring all his life.

I learned I had CLL (Chronic Lymphocytic Leukemia), a blood cancer, in October of 2014. I went through the same process as Greg — shock, acceptance, and trying to make the best with the cards I was dealt. I felt there was a reason and purpose for what was happening to me, so I decided to accept it and do the best I could. I went through six months of chemotherapy in 2016. The chance of my cancer returning at some point in time is 70%. There is no cure for CLL, just like Parkinson's Disease.

The purpose of the medication and treatment for both Parkinson's and CLL is to extend the quality and length of life for as long as possible. Part of the "medication" is the margin in our lives: eating right, exercising regularly, staying close with family and friends, and for me, my faith in God. Without my Christian faith I do not know where I would be right now nor how I would have made it this far. I can honestly say (but not really explain) that I was in an overwhelming stage of peace during the six months of chemotherapy. My faith got me through it and continues to get me through every day since.

So if you experience an Atomic Event in your life, understand that you truly do have a choice to "take the bull by the horns" (Parkinson's disease, CLL, etc.) and kick it! Every morning we wake up, we can choose to be positive, to not become a victim, and to be thankful every day for the good things in our lives. It's not easy, but it truly is worth it.

A cheerful heart is good medicine,
but a crushed spirit dries up the bones.
Proverbs 17:22

CHAPTER 11

SHAKING THE BUCKET

WILL PARKINSON'S BE YOUR SETBACK
OR YOUR CATALYST?

Parkinson's Disease tends to create the illusion of putting limitations on your life. You rarely hear people with Parkinson's talk about accomplishing something new — now that they have PD — that they did not try to do prior to being diagnosed. When we are told of the many motor, non-motor, and psychological symptoms which we should expect to endure, our minds begin to limit ourselves with what we could possibly accomplish. Remember this acronym? F.E.A.R. — Future Expectations Appear Real.

"You have a disease now, you cannot do this." This negative talk can come both externally from spouses, children, or friends — and internally from your own current attitude, lack of rest, and increased medication level. Your external advisors are looking after your best interest. They truly are concerned about you. They do not want you doing compulsive activities because of certain medicines. Your own internal drives are clearly influenced by your attitude at the time, how rested you feel, and how "On" you feel depending on your energy level.

Your mind often plays the, "What if this happens?" game. "What if your tremor causes you to not be able to do certain things?" "What if your leg muscles 'freeze' at a critical point in your adventure and you cannot continue?" Without knowing it, you are sliding away from an Internal Control mindset where you control what you put effort into — towards an External Control mindset where you just take what the world gives you — which usually is not much.

By consciously reminding yourself of the power you possess through Internal Control, you can turn, "What if this goes wrong?" into, "Well, what if I put my mind to it and accomplish this?"

For example, when I first went to an E3 Conference put on by Parkinson's Association of the Rockies in Colorado, I heard the keynote speaker, Becky Farley, speak about climbing the highest peak on all seven continents after she had been diagnosed with Parkinson's. I thought to myself, "Greg, you live in Colorado with more than 50 mountain peaks over 14,000' high. Let's start to climb one fourteener per year and look down on Parkinson's." To date, I have climbed nine of them! Now, please understand I am in good shape, train to stay fit, and I climb the fourteeners with friends and in groups for safety sake, but I have accomplished my goal and more!

I have learned that implementing a plan takes a lot more effort than developing one. While the physical effort is very demanding (breathing thin air), the psychological impact is huge. When you get to the top of a mountain, it is often cold and always windy. Moreover, once you reach the top you have to hike all the way back down the mountain, which is much harder on your balance then going up. However, the endorphins released by your brain upon accomplishing this goal give you a tremendous euphoric feeling. You have taken on a challenge and met your goal because you have Parkinson's, not in spite of it, and that gives you hope!

One of my best friends passed away in his mid-50s during 2018 from an unknown disease. He was an amazing athlete and incredibly strong. The disease that took his life — they never did specifically identify it — acted like ALS or Lou Gehrig's disease. The harsh, sad truth was he never had any personal hope of recovery or even managing life with the mysterious disease. I often think of him when I am climbing mountains or going through the other items on my bucket List. It's comforting to know he did have hope in God, which is why I know I will see him on the basketball courts of heaven.

What might your bucket list look like? Once you understand your reaction to various symptoms and learn to recognize the signs of those conditions coming on, you are in a better position to push yourself towards accomplishing some goals, as you learn to modify your activities to your natural biorhythms. Personally, I am "On" in the morning from 4:00 am to 10:00 am. You should also take into account pharmaceutical fluctuations. If you are mindful and plan ahead, you can avoid troubled times and go stand on top of the world!

I find that checking off life-time bucket list items gives me a large dose of serotonin each time. It also reinforces a positive outlook. I hope that I can still accomplish even more things in life with my Parkinson's.

MODEL:
PARADIGM CUBE

On the next page you will find another visual game. It's called the Paradigm Cube. A paradigm is a pattern of thinking or a mode of being. The following puzzle will challenge your initial way of seeing things, and it will temporarily change your paradigm of vision.

How many different ways can this cube be facing forward at the same time? To help you see differently, name the letters that form the bottom of the cube. Do you see the bottom as BGHC?, DFHC? or AEGB? It all depends on your point of view. Try to see it in all three perspectives.

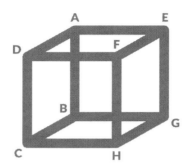

How we look at Parkinson's is similar to how we perceive this object. A paradigm is a shared view of underlying methodology used to understand and categorize various objects. Our brains have so much sensory input in the course of a day, that after a while, we start to categorize things we see and just lump them into a common use or attribute.

Albert Einstein said, "The significant problems we face cannot be solved at the same level of thinking we were at when we created them."[26] This is true as it relates to dealing with the Atomic Events which occur in life. We have to be ready to change our view or paradigm about issues in order to stay one step ahead of the troubles that come with life.

Often, paradigm changes in life are due to an increased level of thinking. We take some time to learn more about a certain object or situation, then re-categorize our thinking about that object or situation. The more comfortable we are with a subject, the stronger our paradigms are. We know what we know. Unfortunately, as the saying goes, "There is no such thing as intelligence; only varying degrees of ignorance." No one knows everything, so we have to keep our minds open to changing our view or paradigm of life, especially when faced with Atomic Events.

I will give you a real-life example of a paradigm shift. I have two friends from high school, Les and Kevin, who have been trying to get me to go elk hunting with them for the last 35 years. Unfortunately, elk season is in mid-November, when the average nighttime low temperature is anywhere from 0-10 degrees Fahrenheit, and the camp they use is at an elevation of 10,500', making it even colder! Cold temperatures have an exaggerated, negative impact on my Parkinson's symptoms, especially my tremors. Once I get cold, I start to shake to the point of it becoming almost uncontrollable. It takes a long time to warm myself back up and stop shaking. This is not conducive to the steadiness required for firing a rifle.

I am also not much of a gun guy to start with, and I had never shot any firearm previously except a .22 rifle at Boy Scout camp decades ago. I was also not too keen on hunting in general as it seemed unfair to me that we would have guns and the elk would not.

Further, that time of the year traditionally was very busy for me at work. It would be nearly impossible to take off 10 days to go elk hunting near Gunnison, Colorado, which is on the other side of the state from where I live on the Front Range. More importantly, my life focus was mostly on working hard and making money for my family. Along came my Atomic Event which drastically affected my life paradigm. I had changed my life purpose from solely being successful in my career to living a significant life with an overriding theme of positivity.

With all of this on my mind, I called Les and asked if I could join in this year's hunt. He was elated! We worked out the hunting license and tags, but decided not to tell our other friend, Kevin, until the morning we left to go hunting. We picked up Kevin about 3:30 am, and I hid under a blanket in the back seat. Les asked Kevin during the morning small talk if there was anyone Kevin wished could have joined them in their elk hunting adventure. Kevin said he couldn't think of anyone. I jumped out from under the blanket and shouted, "What about me?"

His eyes were the size of silver dollars! Hunting turned out to be a great time. The beauty of the mountains, laughter of campfire stories, and camaraderie of the hunters all pitching in to set up camp, haul firewood, and accomplish other chores made for a lifetime of memories. By the way, now after two seasons of hunting, the score is: Greg with his gun 0, Elk 2.

My paradigm of hunting had changed dramatically. It became more about spending time with close friends than the actual act of hunting. I realized that elk are far smarter than I am and no one respects and cares for wildlife like hunters. Hunters who purchase tags to legally hunt, fund +80% of the wildlife management income, which game and fish departments use to improve habitat for the very animals they hunt.

RISE POINT:
CHOOSE YOUR NEW PARADIGM

Parkinson's Disease will want to rob you of your Internal Locus of Control via your own or others' concern for you, but keep your eyes on the horizon. Do not let Parkinson's keep you from pursuing your bucket list items. The natural power generated in your brain and body by tackling new and bigger challenges helps keep a good perspective on Parkinson's. Go to new places and try to do new things, even things you do not think you can do. The view is worth it.

VANTAGE POINT:

KEVIN PETERSEN,
HIGH SCHOOL FRIEND

I played team sports at a small college in the Pacific Northwest. It was there I was introduced to the concept of Intrinsic (internal) and Extrinsic (external) mindsets. As I look at life now, it is about having a Positive Mental Attitude (PMA). Our legendary football coach, Forrest Westering aka "Frosty", championed PMA all the time. His success on the field, and his building quality men and women around him are not debatable. This PMA was part of the entire sports culture at Pacific Lutheran University.

At that time, there was an NBA team in Seattle, the Supersonics. The Sonics had a small (as compared to the other really tall players) point guard on the team named "Slick" Watts. He was around 6' tall, had a slick shaved head, and wore a team colored headband. Slick was quite a character and player. He was also a team motivator. While Slick was not the team mascot, he was part of a caricature drawing that became a true mantra for my understanding of PMA, related to Intrinsic and Extrinsic mindset.

The illustration had 6' Slick driving to the basket facing a 7' giant guarding it. With a fierce and determined look on his face, these words were written under his feet as if they were a trampoline he was bouncing off of, "I CAN BECAUSE I THINK I CAN!" He did not let the extrinsic noise control his intrinsic mindset. In 1976, he led the NBA in steals and assists and was named to the NBA defensive first team.

The mind is very POWERFUL! I am NOT a psychiatrist, but I do believe we can impact the outcome of our lives by understanding and implementing the principle of a PMA mindset. This is how I comprehend the principle: the mind consists of three separate arenas, similar to parts of a computer: 1) the subconscious mind is similar to the hard drive; 2) the creative subconscious mind is like the mouse; 3) the conscious mind is akin to the printer.

Every single piece of information (stimuli) we are exposed to — which we feel, hear, see, speak, or think — is stored on our hard drive. When faced with a needed or requested action, the mouse allows us to access the hard drive for the relevant data concerning the action. Once that data is found, the mouse enables us to send the information to the printer, which then acts to produce the product or outcome. The great news is that we have a minute-by-minute opportunity to impact what negative or positive information is stored on our hard drive. What do we watch? To what and to whom do we listen? What do we say to others, and more importantly, to ourselves?

My friend, Greg, has always been a mentor to me as a living example of PMA. I hope he can keep sharing himself with the world, and I mean not just the Parkie world. We ALL have Atomic Events that occur, which need constant education on how to allow our intrinsic mindset to be filled with, "I can!", to always win the game of life every day.

The scripture in Philippians does not say, "I might not be able to do all things..." It says, I can do all things through Christ who strengthens me. I concur! Make your bucket list and believe you can accomplish it. With PMA, you can impact the world!

I can do all this through Him who gives me strength.
Phillipians 4:13

CHAPTER 12

DEEPER TRUTH

LAYING A FOUNDATION THAT WILL LAST

I want to make sure that with all the discussion about Internal Locus of Control, Response-Ability, and C.O.O.R.E., I establish that the true source of energy for me in dealing with Parkinson's Disease comes from my faith in God. Your mind is a powerful force for healing. You are more than what you eat, think, or do. You are — to a large degree — what you believe you are. "If you think you can, or if you think you can't, you are right".

A strong faith in a spiritual being is a part of your emotional therapy. Many people falsely think that a belief in God will get you a free pass from trials in life, especially Atomic Events. Nothing could be further from the truth. We enjoy lives of free will; we are not puppets. Everyone receives talents and abilities to use in our lives. It is up to each individual to recognize these gifts and use them appropriately to be an example to others. The wiser I get with age and life experience, the more I realize that my life is not about me. It is more about my God-given ability to influence others for good and to play a significant part in their life.

If we believe that God has a plan for our lives, we can envision a future and a hope despite the fact that we have run into an Atomic Event. Hope is derived from character, and character is gained by persevering through a number of trials. We should see our perseverance as providing comfort to others. Then, we can intellectually find the value in dealing with our trials. Our lives are not "falling apart", rather they are "falling into place". It all depends on perspective. Our spiritual mind may be at ease through our faith, but how does this work in our bodies?

Theater of the Mind

There is a phenomenon called the placebo effect in which the brain sees enough outside influences to believe that a certain effect is eminent. Powerful expectations are created in our mind of a certain outcome being true. Our brain believes this input and starts to produce a neurochemical response in our bodies. This is the exact same effect that taking a placebo drug produces on our bodies. Belief produces experience; experience produces neurochemical response; neurochemical response produces feelings in the body; feelings reinforce beliefs; and you have started the positive flywheel of momentum.

Your belief in some positive experience then looks for additional contributing evidence to further support the belief in the placebo. That is why — in the pharmaceutical world — brand name placebos work better than generic labeled placebos. The more involved you are in the Theater of the Mind, the more potent the placebo effect. Fake pills produce a stronger placebo effect than fake creams; injections outperform pills; and surgeries surpass injections.

In addition, the more effort you put into receiving the placebo, the stronger the effect will be. People who make a religious pilgrimage of healing to a known spiritual place often experience stronger healing placebo effects in their bodies than people who merely take a pill. The brain's ability to create a strong belief in your mind, enables your brain to release other neurochemicals produced in your body naturally. Serotonin, dopamine, and cannabinoids are all examples of these neurochemicals that have calming and healing effects. That is why a placebo response travels from the brain to the injury, which is the exact opposite pathway of pain sensation. A positive placebo expectation response in your prefrontal cortex signals to your brain stem to release opioids, which travel down the spinal column to soothe the affected area.

Finally, the power of group thinking by the group of believers who witness the placebo's healing, can further strengthen the belief in the placebo. The communal strength of positive peer pressure can increase the believer's desire to appease the group's thinking and reinforces the positive impact of the placebo.

MODEL:
PARABLE OF THE TALENTS

Parables are stories with a meaning or purpose behind them. That is why Jesus Christ used so many of them while teaching His disciples and the large crowds who gathered to hear Him speak. Matthew 25:14-30 tells one of the great parables of the Bible previously included at the end of *Chapter Seven*, "The Talents".

The landowner mentioned is God, who gives His workers (us) His property to use and develop. God clearly gives differing numbers of talents to various people based upon what they can handle. In the parable, one servant received five talents, another servant received two talents, and still another servant just got one talent. Verse 15 states, *To one he gave five bags of gold, to another two bags, and to another one bag, each according to his ability.* God knows what we are capable of, far better than we will ever know. The servant who received five talents quickly traded with them and gained five more talents. Notice the servant, by trading with the talents, had to take a risk with the landowner's property, but it paid off. The servant who received two talents, did the same thing as the servant with five talents, only on a smaller scale, and ended up with two additional talents. However, the servant who received only one talent did not want to risk losing it, hence buried it in the ground (did not invest or trade it) leaving it there until the landowner returned.

Verse 19 states, *After a long time* — God does not promise us that Atomic Events will clear up quickly — *and settled accounts with them.* The servant with the five original talents went first and he returned the five original talents plus five additional talents, which greatly pleased the landowner. *Well done, good and faithful servant! You have been faithful with a few things; I will put you in charge of many things. Come and share your master's happiness!* Notice that the landowner (master) did not say "Go ahead and keep the talents and retire", instead he said, *I will put you in charge of many things.* The joy in the servant's life (ours) is in daily use of the talents to please the master (God).

The landowner then proceeded to have the same conversation with the second servant as the first, with the same proportional results.

Then, the servant with one talent came to declare that his fear of the landowner as being a hard man caused him to just hide his talent and not earn anything additional for the landowner. The landowner calls him, *wicked, lazy servant!* and says he could have at least loaned out the one talent to earn some interest. The one talent is taken from him and the servant is thrown into the *darkness* where there is *weeping and gnashing of teeth.*

The moral of the story is that the landowner (God) gives everyone (us) differing amounts and types of talents, but He expects everyone to use those talents, over time, to bring Him more talents, to reach other people, and this effort should be the joy of our lives.

"Why would a good God allow you to develop Parkinson's and cut short your effectiveness in life, let alone having to deal with the symptoms of this terrible disease?" I have been asked this question hundreds of times since I was diagnosed. My answer to it may surprise you. Parkinson's Disease has made me far more effective in my life and has greatly expanded my sphere of influence in other people's lives. This brings me great JOY!

Do not get me wrong. Living with the myriad of degenerative effects of Parkinson's Disease in my life is the greatest trial I have ever faced. There is no question that I will most likely live a shorter life span; not be able to work full-time for as long as I had planned; and spend a lot more money and time seeking medical care for my disease than if I did not have PD. I am anxious about what the future progression of the disease will do to my body and how much of a burden I will become on my wife and loved ones. I fear not being able to love my wife as much as she will have to love me by caring for my debilitating body.

One of the direct results of Parkinson's Disease in my life is the shift in my focus. It has moved me away from being a successful Warlord of Commerce to becoming a person who wants to make a significant contribution towards helping others afflicted with PD. I have joined with other like-minded people to start a Parkinson's Community Center in the Denver, Colorado metro area, called Parkinson's Pointe. PD is not a very large disease (based on the number of people afflicted with it), so to date it has not received much attention from the medical or other communities. No such Parkinson's Disease specific facility exists in my region, and there are only three facilities that deal with PD in this format across our nation.

I have previous professional experience in creating, building, and developing three different companies into strong business enterprises. I was asked to help establish a Board of Directors for Parkinson's Pointe based on that previous work experience and my involvement serving on other boards.

How interesting that all these experiences, and my abilities to fulfill them, showed up in my life right before they were needed to get Parkinson's Pointe to become more than just a dream. The convergence of Parkinson's exploding as a disease on a global scale, the need it creates regionally, my diagnosis of the disease after learning the life lessons I have, strikes me as providentially directed and purposeful.

There is another well known parable in the bible, one about "the good soil", it comes from Mathew 13:8. Jesus explains that people are a lot like soil, and that God's word is like a seed. Depending on how well each type of soil can accept and nurture the seed, some soils have the potential to multiply 30, 60, or even 100 times the investment of the sower.

I don't know about you, but I truly want my legacy to be the 100X kind. Parkinson's has been a real hardship for both myself and also those around me, and it will continue to be a growing challenge for the rest of my life. But I have learned that difficulties can be used to either harden our hearts or cultivate our souls for the better depending on how well we handle them. My job is to be receptive of the necessary tilling, so that I can receive the seeds of life and make them grow exponentially over time. I want to multiply the talents and seeds that I have received from the sower by a factor of 100.

My faith enables me to see that my season of life dealing with PD has a far bigger influence on my wife, children, grandchildren, friends, and co-workers than my life did pre-Parkinson's. They are watching me like hawks to see if I can stay true to my faith and find the peace that passes all understanding. I have been devoted to Scripture memorization since my college years; now people want to see if I can live what I proclaim.

Fortunately, my landowner, Jesus, is here for me every step of the way. It is only through His strength that I have the ability to live my life daily in a fashion that hopefully pleases Him. I know for certain that when I am done dealing with Parkinson's in my life, I will hear the words, "Well done, good and faithful servant",[27] and I relish the idea of having a new, heavenly body

---

RISE POINT:
GOD'S PLAN SHOULD BE YOUR PLAN

The sooner you make God's plan for your life, your plan for your life, the sooner you will be able to experience the peace that passes all understanding. The following Bible verses should be read in this order. They have been selected to help you answer the question, "Why would a good God allow you to develop Parkinson's Disease in your life?"

1. *Not only so, but we also glory in our sufferings, because we know that suffering produces perseverance; perseverance, character; and character, hope* (Romans 5:3-4).

2. *I consider that our present sufferings are not worth comparing with the glory that will be revealed in us* (Romans 8:18).

3. *The Lord will fight for you; you need only to be still* (Exodus 14:14).

4. *So do not fear, for I am with you; do not be dismayed, for I am your God. I will strengthen you and help you; I will uphold you with my righteous right hand* (Isaiah 41:10).

5. *I always thank my God for you because of His grace given you in Christ Jesus* (I Corinthians 1:4).

6. *"For I know the plans I have for you," declares the Lord, "plans to prosper you and not to harm you, plans to give you hope and a future. Then you will call on me and come and pray to me, and I will listen to you. You will seek me and find me when you seek me with all your heart"* (Jeremiah 29:11-13).

VANTAGE POINT:

DR. MICHAEL A.L. ECKELKAMP, *LEAD PASTOR, ST. JOHN'S LUTHERAN CHURCH, DENVER, COLORADO*

There are many different words that I could use to describe Greg. Some are appropriate for a book, others are up for debate. I seriously doubt anyone else would use the word "chairbler" to describe him! This now defunct term from the 17th century refers to furniture builders, and in this case, one specializing in making chairs.

A chairbler knows that, because of the design of our hips, a chair with four legs provides comfort. An added benefit is that if one leg is not functioning, a four-legged chair is still useful.

Greg has a remarkable strength about him because he focuses on four "legs" for the "chair" of his life. Each leg is different yet interdependent. They depend on each other in a symbiotic fashion. The names of the four legs of Greg's chair are "body", "mind", "spirit", and "family".

Greg often refers to managing an Atomic Event. Greg's "Nucflash" is Parkinson's. He is a life-long learner, intensely focused on making his "chair" strong. While his body is gradually growing weak, he is focused on mitigating the weight load of his "shaky legs" on his body by strengthening his mind, spirit, and family. Greg celebrates what the Psalmist announces, *I praise you because I am fearfully and wonderfully made; your works are wonderful, I know that full well* (Psalm 139:14).

Greg refuses to bury his talent in the ground (Matthew 25:25). Similar to the distributed strength of a four-legged chair with only three 100% functional legs, he is living his life in a way that both depends on and further strengthens his mind, spirit, and family. Greg is investing the remainder of his earthly life in that which matters for eternity. He will only have Parkinson's for a while on earth, but by investing his life in his other "chair legs", he is building for that which is eternal in Heaven.

"His master replied, 'Well done, good and faithful servant! You have been faithful with a few things; I will put you in charge of many things. Come and share your master's happiness!
Matthew 25:21

CHAPTER 13

EXERCISE

THE GREAT ELIXIR

With medical science currently unable to crack the code of Parkinson's Disease, somebody has got to do something for all those afflicted, to help them better cope with this disease physically. So far, we have talked about support teams, overcoming fear, prescription drugs, changing paradigms, problem solving, and much more. You want to know what works for me the best? Pure and simple: exercise!

Discussions on neuroplasticity, sarcopenia, or pharmacological reactions are all important, but if I want to feel good right now, I go work out.

Everyone's Parkinson's symptoms are different and so is everyone's ability to exercise. You have to find out what works for you. Do you like to run or walk, dance or bike, do yoga or Tai Chi? Whatever it is, just do it!

Sarcopenia is a syndrome found in older people. It is associated with loss of muscle mass, strength, and overall performance. These lead to increased incidence of falls, movement impairment, and disability. Many factors play into the development of Sarcopenia, but disuse, changing endocrine function, inflammation, and nutritional deficiencies are certainly key factors. Loss of muscle mass and strength — when combined with increased body weight — leads to additional strains on physical performance. Reduction in the production of testosterone and estrogen, which coincide with aging, appear to accelerate sarcopenia's development.

Physical activity generally declines with age. A third of Americans between the ages of 65-74, and half of those over the age of 75 are inactive. It is time to get up and get moving!

The pharmaceuticals prescribed for treatment of the symptoms of Parkinson's Disease are potent drugs that often have strong iatrogenic[28] effects on you. The negative side effects of taking these drugs can impact your attitude, behavior, and outlook on life, in addition to the physical effects on your body. Nature has an answer for those of us with PD. It's a natural pharmacy found in your body, and this pharmaceutical is called, exercise. Given the proper effort and duration of exercise, your brain produces several beneficial chemicals such as endorphins, serotonin, and opioids.

Exercise at any level brings about beneficial impacts on your heart and blood pressure, reduces fatigue, and improves attitude. Just as there are many levels of Parkinson's, there are many levels of ability to exercise, and all of them bring about positive effects. It is never too late to start exercising!

Your exercise program should include balance, cardio-respiratory, strength, and stretching exercises. Be sure to start slowly — especially if you have not been exercising recently — and always check with your doctor regarding any health issues you have before you start a new

---

[28] Iatrogenic, adjective, iat·ro·gen·ic, ī-,a-trə-'je-nik. Induced inadvertently by a physician or surgeon or by medical treatment or diagnostic procedures. *Merriam-Webster*. Retrieved 2.6.20 from https://www.merriam-webster.com/dictionary/iatrogenic.

exercise regime. If you choose to work out at a gym or other facility, you often will also develop a sense of community or belonging to a group, which is another important positive result.

Proper exercise — by boosting metabolism, improving physical body functions, and heightening mood — is seen as offering neuroprotective properties to your nervous system. Be sure to set realistic goals for yourself. I have found working with a physical therapist is ideal in that the therapist knows my capabilities and pushes me to do better over time, but also knows my limitations. Ideally, you want to get your heart rate up to the "talk test" level. That is where you work out hard enough to break a sweat, yet you are still able to have a conversation. Often this is around 50%-60% of your maximum heart rate. As you improve your stamina, you can move this up toward the 80% range.

As with any new activity — like learning to ski or playing the piano — it is best if you get guidance from a professional instructor (trainer) when you first start your exercise regimen. They will help show you the proper form and duration of the various exercises and the safe use of equipment. Scheduling the optimal time of day and location for exercise will help you pass the "21-day test" of developing a behavior or routine. It is said that 80% of New Year resolutions are over by the 20th day. Keeping focused on improvement and having fun with whom you are exercising, are other keys to developing a habit of exercise. Music is another element that helps turn exercise into a fun activity. It is amazing to me how listening to certain music, with a particular beat, can enhance my workout and endurance.

Riding a tandem bike and boxing drills with a workout partner are two examples of what is termed "forced-exercise" activities. Forced-exercise is when you exercise with another person who works out at a higher level than you, thus forcing you to work out at a higher rate than your normal, preferred rate. This method of exercise is seen as a friendly way of pushing yourself to a new level of fitness, while enjoying the company of another person.

How does a person with Parkinson's Disease use exercise to improve their lives? When exercising, you are using your brain and body in new ways, thus creating new, alternative brain (neural) pathways to get your body to move. This is called "neuroplasticity". This is the improvement of brain function by enhancing the development of new nerve connections to perform a specific task. As you age, or if you have PD, you start to lose the nerve-firing pathways you created as a child or young adult. Exercise can help you develop new pathways to handle the movement of your body. You learned balance as a child, what is to prevent you from learning it again as an adult? The difference is that you have no memory of all the falling and near-misses you experienced as a young child. Now as an adult, you will have to rationalize your desire to learn a new sense balance over the fear of hurting yourself.

Not all exercise is of value. Exercise needs to meet certain criteria — such as walking at least 10,000 steps per day — in order to have neuroplasticity characteristics. Balance, dual or triple tasking, intensity of heart rate, and range of motion all play a key role in determining the value of the exercise you do. As your brain and body move, you are building new pathways for your body to function. Think of it as rewiring your brain. You are forcing your body to boost its ability to stay in the game.

MODEL:
PHYSICAL EXERCISE

Exercise should have several characteristics to be effective. Aerobic exercise is designed to get your heart rate up into the 150-160 maximum heart rate beats-per-minute range, if you are in decent shape and are between the age of 57 to 74. You should always check with your doctor before starting any new cardiovascular exercise program. Any exercise that gets you to 50% or higher of your age appropriate beats-per-minute, for at least 10 minutes, is considered quality exercise. Remember to "walk before you run", both figuratively and literally. Boxing appears to be a great form of exercise that combines both aerobic and balance improvements for those of us with Parkinson's Disease. I like to think of boxing as my ability to beat the crap out of Parkinson's!

Balance exercises are particularly important for those with PD, because the disease is constantly attacking your postural stability and muscle stiffness. Yoga and Tai Chi can help your body relearn balance, both visually and through your vestibular system (inner ear). Both of those exercise types also aid in improving your flexibility and stretching by reducing muscle stiffness and improved range of motion. The cognitive function of "flowing" through your classes also aids in tying the physical exertion and mental well-being of your mind by releasing the natural chemicals we have already discussed.

Weight and resistance exercise is another important component to any good workout regimen. It is important to track the actual weight/ intensity of your exercise and the maximum number of repetitions — done correctly — to work the various types of muscle cells in your body. My normal body weight is around 172 lbs. If I were working my chest muscles via bench pressing, and I want to build slow-twitch muscle cells for endurance, I would use a high number of repetitions (12-15) at 65% of my maximum (225 lbs.) or 145 lbs. If I wanted to increase the intensity — to build more fast-twitch muscles cells — I would drop the number of reps to 8-10 at 75% of my maximum or 170 lbs. If I was seeking to obtain maximum muscle cell development, I would need to drop the number of reps to 3-5 at 90% of my maximum or 205 lbs.

Finally, if I was feeling particularly strong that day and wanted to show off to my grandsons, I might try to hoist 225 lbs. one time. It is very common when you first get back to lifting weights to see some quick growth in your maximum weight lifting abilities, but then you usually plateau out at a weight that is commensurate with your body type and weight. For example, most non-exercisers have a hard time lifting their actual body weight just once. If you stick with your exercise plan you can quickly get to the point where you can do your body weight for ten reps, then your maximum one-time lift weight might be your body weight plus 10%.

Muscle confusion is another method of exercise that has you perform new and different exercises. These often combine mental and physical demands on you, thus your brain and body have to burn in new neural pathways for a particular movement. We have trillions of nerves in our brain and body; let's use them all to help beat Parkinson's at its own game.

It is important to also remember that sleep, relaxation, diet, and nutrition — while not actually exercise — all play a vital role in enhancing your exercise program and your body's ability to recover from the workouts faster and more completely. I find that working out improves my appetite; improves my GI functioning; and helps me to sleep better than on days I do not exercise.

RISE POINT:
COMMIT TO AN EXERCISE LIFESTYLE

Proper exercise that is doctor approved and professionally programmed, has neuro-protective attributes. Exercise that develops neuroplasticity over time includes aerobic, balance, cardiovascular, flexibility, and strength components. If you commit to spending the time it takes to exercise — and adding proper diet, nutrition, relaxation, and sleep to your lifestyle — I believe you can hold off the effects of Parkinson's in your brain and body. By the way, the "drugs" you get for your brain from exercising are free!

VANTAGE POINT:

MINDY HEIMER,
DAUGHTER

I always thought my dad was stronger than Superman!

My family loved to hang a bunch of pictures around the house from all the adventures we took together. My favorites were the pictures of the trips my Mom and Dad took before my sisters and I were born. He was always shirtless and flexing in every picture taken by a lake or a beach and man, he was ripped! And as you can guess from the contents of this chapter, he still is. We spend a lot of time at the lake during the summer on our stand up paddleboards. When Dad is there with MY young children, he often gets complimented on how cute HIS "sons" are.

Being physically, emotionally, and mentally fit have always been things I have seen my dad, Greg, strive to do. Just like when he speaks with others, in this book Dad brings up some wonderful advice about ways to get started exercising, reminding readers to check with their doctor before they do, and what exercises are best for Parkies. Although, he left out my favorite ... dancing!

There's a lot of research emerging about Parkinson's Disease and exercise. There's even more research showing the importance of community while exercising. Dad did a great job covering the nitty-gritty of all of that, but I want to take a moment to help you unfold one little word: Why?

Why start exercising? Why start working out after you've been diagnosed with Parkinson's Disease? Why should we all take our physical health seriously? When you start to answer the "Why?" of those questions, a lot of answers may brew to the surface. "I want to reach this certain size clothing in six months." "I have a vacation coming up and I hate how this dress looks on me." "I'm tired of what I see in the mirror."

When I started taking my health seriously, I had just had my second son. It was then that I learned about Creeping Obesity. On average, American adults will gain anywhere from 5-15 lbs. each year, most without noticing. It's a simple multiplication math equation to figure out how much you'll weigh as the years go by. It was 2012 and I was at my heaviest (177 lbs. — I'm 5'6"). With two young boys, I started to mentally add up how big that number on the scale would be by the time they graduated high school. I wasn't thrilled about it! But there was something deep inside me that kept rearing its ugly head and telling me I wasn't worth it and even if I wanted to change, I would never be able to. I had tried in the past, failed miserably, so why try again?

In the past, my "Why?" had always been surface level. Those answers I previously listed above were my actual answers — what I thought were my "Why's?". One day, I caught myself tearing down another woman (whom I didn't even know) because she had the body type I wanted. I can't write out the words that I called her, because I'm pretty sure my Mom and Dad would still ground me if they read it! It truly was an out-of-body experience and I asked myself, "What if you said those things out loud?" "How would that make her feel?" "Does it make you a better person?" Obviously, the answer to that last question was "No!".

So, for Lent (the 40-day season of reflection and preparation preceding Easter) that year I gave up negativity. I didn't allow myself to talk negatively about other people or about myself. And let me tell you, that was the hardest thing I have ever done! Run a half marathon? Piece of cake. Give birth? Easy peasy. Give up negative self-talk? It's like learning to walk all over again while blindfolded and hung upside down. I needed something to redirect my thoughts. Enter my mantra. A mantra is a word or phrase used to help focus your meditation or mind. My mantra was simple, "God made me strong and beautiful because I am worth it." Those words speak deep into my soul. I Corinthians 6:19-20 reminds us we should honor God by treating our bodies as His temple where the Holy Spirit resides.

As the days went by, and as I kept breathing through my mantra anytime those negative thoughts came, my mind started to clear up. I was able to really understand why I wanted to change my physical health. I want to be around to watch my boys graduate. I want to play with them and not get tired. I want to look hot for my husband! I want to set a good example for anyone who watches me. Once my "Why?" had some true value to it, exercising became the easy part. Over the next seven months, I lost 40 lbs. and it changed my life forever. I found God's call in my life — to help people through exercise — and I found my new purpose in life. You can, too!

I know that sometimes reading other people's stories about their fitness journeys and successes can cause past hurts to resurface. And I know that you are now on a new journey in life that you hadn't anticipated taking. But I do know one thing to be true: you are worth every moment of every workout you have done and will do. You have what it takes to be strong again. You can do this. And there's a community of people waiting to come alongside you.

Talk with your doctor about which exercise is best for you, and do some research on where you can go to find like-minded people who are on your same journey. Whatever you do, don't stop this dance called life. You've been given a chance to learn some new dance moves, so find a new rhythm to get lost in and a new beat to walk to. Just because the song changed doesn't mean your dance is over.

By the way, I know my dad is even stronger than Superman. So are you!

Do you not know that your bodies are temples of the Holy Spirit, who is in you, whom you have received from God? You are not your own; you were bought at a price. Therefore honor God with your bodies.
1 Corinthians 6:19-20

MINDY AND GREG

DOING YOGA ON A STREET IN DOWNTOWN DENVER

CHAPTER 14

GET S.M.A.R.T.

SPECIFIC, MEASURABLE, ACHIEVABLE,
REALISTIC, TIMELY

We all know that everyone's Parkinson's Disease symptoms are different. That is why it is important to continually monitor and assess your treatment plan on at least a yearly basis. Later, I will show you a model I use to annually assess what is working in my battle with Parkinson's.

Everybody needs a number one line of defense, or "go to" activity to help keep your attitude and energy level up on those especially bad Parkinson's symptoms days. I have found that together, physical exercise and yoga are my number one line of defense. Sure, nutrition, medication, and supplements help, but when I need to start my day right or am just having a bad symptom day — I go straight to exercise — especially with my support group people.

There are both physiological and psychological reasons this works for me. First, when you work out with a group of people over a long period of time — like my 6 am Yoga Fit class — you develop a sense of belonging to that group. Everyone is there trying to do what the instructor has planned for that day. A certain sense of comradery kicks in and you get a sense of belonging while accomplishing something together. This is Net Forward Energy at its best! Serotonin is streaming through your brain, and your life looks a whole lot happier. You also get a second shot of feel good medicine when your body starts to produce naturally occurring endorphins and opioids from your physical effort. This is a powerful double dose of symptom fighting medicine with little to no negative side effects.

My middle daughter, Mindy, works in ministry doing this exact thing. She provides a Health and Wellness Ministry through a church to the surrounding community. She teaches Holy Yoga, Re-Fit, and other Christian-based physical activities. This combines yet a third positive element — faith — which we talked about in *Chapter Twelve*.

After I was first diagnosed with PD, Mindy held a "Dance-A-Thon" the following April (Parkinson's Awareness month). This allowed me to collect the donated funds as a contribution to Parkinson's of the Rockies, a local association dedicated to improving the lives of Parkies. She and her group raised close to $2,000.00 on a Saturday morning by simply doing a wide variety of dance exercises.

Mindy continues to support me through various races and events. She was my team leader when I participated in Pedaling 4 Parkinson's. She drove ahead of me to be at every rest stop with nutrition, fluids, and encouraging words for the 40-mile tandem bike ride which raised money for Parkinson's. Each May, we run together as a family in the Bolder Boulder, the third largest 10 K on-road foot race in America. There is no greater sense of accomplishment than at the end of that race when we run together into the University of Colorado's Folsom Stadium — to the roar of 50,000 people — and each do a cartwheel as we approach the finish line!

More importantly, for the first time since I was diagnosed with PD, I realized that myself and those who were in my support group of family and friends could do something about beating Parkinson's. That gave me hope! Remember, Romans 5:3-4 tells us we should, *glory in our sufferings, because we know that suffering produces perseverance; perseverance, character; and character, hope.* We all know what our minds can do with hope!

I mentioned my friend Steve in *Chapter Five*. He has been my climbing buddy when I have attempted to climb at least one 14,000' high mountain each summer since I was diagnosed. It is exciting to see the world from the top of a mountain, but even more so when you know that you not only carried your backpack up to the top, but you carried Parkinson's Disease along with it.

If you do not have family or friends to help push you to achieve new levels of fitness, try working with one of the Parkinson's support groups you might have in your area. In Colorado, we are fortunate to have several strong and active associations to connect with for getting involved in a wide-range of activities. These are designed to improve your well being and share a sense of community.

We have an organization named, The Unsteady Hand, that promotes an improved quality of life for people with Parkinson's through Communal Creative Engagement. Monthly Creativity Labs are an opportunity to focus on a purposeful activity and engage your creative spirits.

The Parkinson's Association of the Rockies (PAR) connects and empowers people with Parkinson's to thrive through education by offering professionally conducted classes in art, boxing, dance, exercise, and spinning. PAR also offers great programs and symposiums, such as E3, that are designed to Educate, Energize, and Empower. Sessions at E3 bring you up to speed on research, caregiver information, and local support group opportunities.

The Davis Phinney Foundation is a non-profit organization dedicated to helping people with Parkinson's live life well. Davis, who was an Olympic medal-winning cyclist, started his Foundation to help people thrive in spite of their PD. The Davis Phinney Foundation is international in scope, and has one of the best information manuals, *Every Victory Counts,* which covers almost every facet of living with Parkinson's. They also have a large inventory of videos and webinars on a broad range of subjects that are very informative.

The Michael J. Fox Foundation is a large organization started by that actor after he was diagnosed with Parkinson's. They focus their energies on research and have an outstanding online portal called, *Fox Insight*, which is designed to offer virtual research opportunities that anyone, anywhere can participate in. *Fox Trial Finder* is designed for people who want to be agents of change by actively searching for clinical trials in their geographical area, which interest them.

The Parkinson's Foundation is another international organization designed to make life better for people with Parkinson's by improving care and advancing research toward a cure. They offer a number of videos, webinars, manuals, and consolations all designed to help make sure the people with Parkinson's have been heard.

Check in your community to see if there is a local branch of one of these national organizations. It is well worth the effort. The *Endnotes* section of this book lists the name and contact information for these PD organizations and more.

MODEL:
PARKINSON'S YEARLY ASSESSMENT

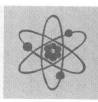

Parkinson's is a hard disease to understand. As I've pointed out before, there are no known biological markers — such as an enzyme in your blood — to monitor its debilitating progress. So, by using strategy tools I learned in running private businesses, I have developed a "Market Share" approach to identifying the various factors that influence my dealing with Parkinson's.

For me, these factors include the obvious ones: doctors, pharmaceuticals, nutrition, and support groups. I have also found another whole set of factors, which carry much more weight in my battle with Parkinson's. These include: alternative therapies, philanthropy, faith-based emotional therapies, exercise, and yoga. There is an example of a worksheet I use with my own answers on the next page.

I started by observing what factors had positive attributes and which ones had negative attributes. In my world, bananas don't help my fight with constipation, even though I love to eat them. Grapefruit juice, on the other hand, though bitter to the taste, seems to work wonders for me. I have tried to narrow the focus of which factors seem most valuable, then leverage those factors in my life to move from "doing" your best with Parkinson's, to "being" your best with Parkinson's. In other words, learning to thrive!

For your own assessment, first start by identifying all sources of aid, or factors, which you have at your disposal. Consider the total cost of procurement, both the costs of acquisition and the costs of possession. Next, you need to monitor these factors for various outcomes. I notice that when I eat a large steak, my medicine wears off sooner and faster; which is not true if I eat the same portion or larger of salmon. Red meat hinders the absorption of levodopa, while omega 3s found in salmon, augment it. The saying goes like this, "No data free discussions; if you cannot measure it, you cannot manage it".

Parkinson's Life Assessment – 2019

Factors I believe help me live successfully with Parkinson's

Hope for _____Summary of _____

Factor:	% of effect	Positives	Negatives
Exercise	14	"control", endorphins	moving
Therapy	14	faith, paddleboard, nature	fighting compulsions
Nutrition	13	CoQ10, D-3, omega 3	less sugar, red meat
Yoga	10	meditation, balance	N/A
Alt. Therapy	10	physical therapy, boxing	backward movements
Supplements	9	Protandim, Selenium	need B complex
Support Group	6	Speak more, 3E's, studies	More PAR/Ski Days
Community	6	you know everyone	travel time
Creativity	6	explore new side of you	tremored hands
Doctors	5	need holistic approach	doesn't know me
Medication	5	carbo/levo	$, pramipexole
Retirement	2	more margin in life	<$; forced into it

100%

Now, force rank each factor against each other, on a scale of 0% impact to 100%. I have identified 12 factors in my battle with Parkinson's, so their collective total impact should be 100%. If you now assign a weight to each factor, it should be like a "Return on Investment" (ROI) assessment of that factor. You might consider such things as costs to join clubs, how much do you have to force yourself to perform the activity, time constraints, and risk of injury.

In my world, I attribute the following life-share percentages to each of the 12 factors I mentioned: alternative therapy 10%; doctors 5%; emotional therapy 14%; exercise 14%; medicines RX 5%; nutrition 13%; supplements 9%; support groups 6%; local community groups 6%; creative expression 6%; retirement 2% and yoga 10%. Now, when you add in the weighted time/cost attribute, you get a clear idea of which factor gives you your best Return on Investment (ROI). A factor with a high time/cost attribute might only get a ROI weight of 0.75, while a medium time/cost attribute would have a ROI weight of 1.0, and a low time/cost attribute would have a ROI weight of 1.25.

For example, the factors of doctors, medicines, and supplements all have a high time/cost attribute, meaning you spend a lot of time performing those tasks and they are very expensive, relative to the effect they are having for improvement in your life with Parkinson's. If supplements had a market share of 9% and a ROI weight of 0.75, then it's actual market share is 6.75%.

The factors of exercise, nutrition, and yoga each have a medium time/cost attribute, which carries a weight of 1.0. Therefore, yoga had a market share of 10% and a ROI weight of 1.0, so it's actual market share is 10%. Finally, the factors of alternative therapy, emotional therapy, and support groups have low a time/cost attribute, which carries a weight of 1.25. Emotional therapy — which includes things like faith; paddle boarding (nature); and speaking/teaching — had a market share of 14%, but rises to a weighted share of 17.5, passing up exercise.

My hope is that by taking subjective feelings and actions, assigning a numerical value to them, I can start building a trackable history of data points to compare with previous years. By building a trend line of several years' worth of data, we can start to notice what areas are improving, stabilizing, or falling. I can even see which factors are waxing or waning in market share over time. This is called Delphi Analysis, where the actual numbers are not so important as the trend line you are trying to manage. This gives a person a sense of control or hope and it feeds your Internal Locus of Control (*Chapter Ten*).

Once you have a history to look at, you can see how things are changing and can alter your perception of the type of change in your life from being Crisis change (the worst) to Evolutionary change, which is seen as easier to deal with (*Chapter Nine*). Once you can see what is working, what is not, and why, you are in a position to develop S.M.A.R.T. goals for your next year's battle with Parkinson's.

By now you have probably noticed how much I appreciate the ability of an acronym to help an important truth stick in our minds. S.M.A.R.T. describes a method of developing goals by which you have an increased chance of accomplishing them. "S" stands for Specific, meaning use actual numbers, dates, units of measure, that everyone agrees to. "M" stands for Measurable, meaning that a group will agree by what unit of measure they will be judged (weighted market share). "A" stands for Achievable, the goal must be believed to be seen as obtainable by the group at the beginning of the goal period. "R" stands for Realistic, meaning the group must see the valid reason for having the goal. It cannot be seen as a whim of the goal setter. "T" stands for Timely, there has to be agreed upon time commitments. For example, "I will speak to four newly diagnosed support groups by the end of the year using my PowerPoint presentation".

The S.M.A.R.T. system helps me stay on track, and it makes for a more efficient return on investment of time and money.

RISE POINT:
DEVELOP A LIFE ASSESSMENT TOOL

In order to build a greater sense of empowerment in dealing with Parkinson's Disease, try developing an annual Life Assessment Tool. Pick the factors you feel are an accurate measure of your progress in dealing with PD. Try assigning a market share percentage number to each factor, the total of which should be 100%. Assign a weighted ROI to each factor's market share, by comparing the time/cost involved with that factor in your life. Monitor these on a yearly basis. You might want to assess quarterly when you first start to build a faster trend line. Finally, set S.M.A.R.T. goals for next year's battle with Parkinson's. Good luck and Godspeed!

VANTAGE POINT:

TIM MELCHIOR,
BUSINESS ASSOCIATE

As I walked into a coffee shop for an interview regarding a new job when contemplating a career change, Greg Ritscher was waiting for me. I had not met him prior to this and was warmly greeted with his questions about what my career had looked like up until that point. Then, the interview became different than what I was used to. He began to talk about personality types, and I was handed a series of assessments to take with me to complete and return to him.

A week or so later, I got a call from Greg because he wanted to meet and discuss the assessment results he had reviewed. He also wanted to talk about the possibility of me working for him. In our second meeting, he shared the results with me. This brought clarity to some of the things I was considering and how the pieces of the puzzle would fit together. As we discussed my working for him, I knew it would be a different path than what I was used to. I was hired a couple weeks later by Greg, then had the opportunity to work closely with him for a few years.

I knew Greg had Parkinson's Disease since our first meeting. As I noticed some slight tremors, Greg was very open to talking about PD as if it was just a natural part of his life. I had not known much about Parkinson's up until that point. He told me a little about it, then went on to describe what some of his daily routines were that helped him combat the progression of the disease. I quickly realized Greg was very active, had a purpose for almost everything he did, and he thought through everything well in advance.

Over the next few years, I got to spend a lot of time with Greg. In addition to being his employee, we also shared an office so I got to learn quite a bit about Greg in a short amount of time, both personally and in business. While working together, I observed several of his interactions involving others both within the company and outside of it. He would always tell me, "There should be no data-free meetings."

Greg had researched, studied, knew statistics, and had a purpose for every meeting. Another thing I learned about Greg was that he had an acronym for just about everything. This seemed to help ideas stick with our sales team, keeping us focused on our goals. As a manager, Greg would encourage our team to always be paying attention to customers' needs, watching market trends, staying on top of product knowledge, among other important sales skills. All of this was so we could be the best resource possible for our customers. Every year, we would have strategic meetings to discuss and address these issues for the following year. He encouraged us to have a purpose for the things we did every day, which would result in a positive effect on our business dealings.

I'll always remember meeting people with Greg. They would ask how he was doing; he would usually say, "shaken, not stirred". This immediately opened up the opportunity for anyone to discuss Parkinson's Disease with him. When asked, he would usually describe very candidly some of the issues he was facing and how he was addressing them head-on. In the same way he prepared for work meetings, he collected research, statistics, graphs, and everything else on Parkinson's. This helped him face the challenges, armed with some of the best ways to combat them.

Greg committed himself to executing a plan that would slow down the progression of his Parkinson's Disease. It seemed he always chose a positive attitude about everything. Rather than letting Parkinson's bring him down, he used it to continue to better himself.

While working together, one of the most important things I learned from Greg was to continually do things for work and in life "on purpose". Greg believes without doubt that God put him, you, and me on this earth for a purpose. Let's all go out and make the best of it!

Not only so, but we also glory in our sufferings,
because we know that suffering produces perseverance;
perseverance, character; and character, hope.
Romans 5:3-4

CHAPTER 15

VISION

THE POWER OF SEEING BEYOND

Parkinson's Disease often creates the illusion that you will no longer be able to work effectively or achieve any personal fulfillment through your employment. Few people get the chance to live out the models they learn in life as I have been blessed to do three times in my business career. It is why I am such a strong believer in the power of models. *Chapter Twelve* discussed the power of the Theater of the Mind. Your mind can create a new reality by focusing on the settings, props, and actions of your peers, in order to create a believable future that you bring into your new reality.

Let me tell you about the belief in 50/50 Vision and Metco Landscape. I first met Mark, the owner of Metco Landscape, located in Denver, Colorado, in 1991. He had started Metco in 1986, and like most new landscape contractors, had only grown to $1M in revenue after five years in business.

The seasonality of the landscape industry in Colorado makes it particularly difficult to manage cash flow, and Metco was no exception. I met Mark in a meeting to determine if he was worth extending additional terms of sale to for getting Metco through the challenging winter months. There was something about his character that just told me Mark was worth the risk and he had a passionate belief in his company. As time went on, Mark continued to grow his company, and while he needed help for several more years, Metco was approaching a more stable financial condition with each passing year.

By the fall of 2001, Mark had been in business for 15 years and had grown to $3M in revenues. It was on the Thursday of "9/11" week that Mark called me, frustrated with his business and its demands on his life. I asked him to come up with a vision for his business when we met the following Monday. The book of Proverbs[29] explains how a nation without a vision will perish. The same is true of a company! That is why I asked Mark to develop a vision for Metco. Once a group of people pursuing a shared vision or outcome begin to work together, the power they exert on each other to build a strength called "Net Forward Energy Ratio" (or NEFER for short) is significantly positive.

At that next meeting, Mark described the vision he had come up with for Metco. He termed it the 50/50 goal. He wanted to do $50M dollars in revenue by the time he was 50-years-old. That was an audacious vision in anyone's book! Mark was forty-years-old when he came up with the vision. He had been in business for 15 years, and had grown the company to $3M dollars. Let me also tell you that up to that point in the history of Colorado, no landscape contractor had ever done $50M dollars in revenue in one year. So, this was a huge vision to believe in and pursue. Metco indeed achieved the goal of having over +$50M in revenue in 2016. While this was five years after 2011, his business like others were still fighting uphill against the long term impact of the 2008 Great Recession.

---

[29] Proverbs 29:18

Just like the Theater of the Mind, a number of factors (like settings in a theater) had to come into play in order for Metco to achieve Mark's vision. Demographically, the Baby Boomer's had to be in their prime earning and spending years. Economically, home values started to escalate because of low interest rates and the very tight supply of homes on the market. Abnormally high consumer confidence drove the home-buying desire, and loose credit qualifications expanded the number of house hunters. Environmentally, nature provided abundant snowpack and water supply. All of these factors helped make for very positive housing and associated landscaping business environments.

The 50/50 Vision also helped direct Metco's hiring and personnel decisions, as well as drove their market plans and sales direction (like theater props). After putting the right people in the right seats and building strong systems that could support the increased production capacity of Metco, the results started to gain momentum. Once employees started to see the results, they started to believe that $50M in revenue was achievable (peer pressure). An employee driven vision statement was developed and the workers started to buy into Mark's vision. To date, Metco has exceeded the $50M dollar revenue goal for three consecutive years.

Mark's vision accomplished a number of things: employment for hundreds of workers, an increase in tax revenues for the communities they worked in, and creation of a platform for Metco to become the source of benevolence for a number of organizations helping the underprivileged throughout the greater Denver area. Mark does not like to receive public accolades for his kind heart, but one of the major reasons myself and his co-workers labored so hard for him to achieve his vision was because of his philanthropy!

On a side note, I was able to work on the Board of Directors for an inner city school for disadvantaged children. This was a huge life goal achievement for me which was also excellent for my mental health. One of the best ways to keep a positive attitude about your life is to make someone else's life better for them having interacted with you.

MODEL:
NET FORWARD ENERGY RATIO

Have you ever wondered how group thinking can be such a powerful force in achieving results for an organization? The book *Enlightened Leadership*[30] by Ed Oakley and Doug Krug describes the phenomenon known as "Net Forward Energy Ratio". This model describes how a group of ten people can move from not being aware of an issue, to creating a majority of acceptance, to finally having complete buy-in.

This is really a mathematical model that has psychological emphasis. Once you understand its principles, you will notice it happening in groups around you. Any group that is capable of achieving a stated goal will have the following type of people in it:

Leader – This is the entrepreneur, visionary, or dreamer. You only need one of these high energy, risk-takers to champion an idea. The more charismatic they are, the better.

Second Man In – This is the first person to join the leader in achieving the goal. This is the most important person in the group, often a maven or connector. Leaders by definition need followers. The rest of the people types will never follow a leader on their own, for fear of change (discussed in *Chapter Nine*). It is only when they see a Second Man In align with the Leader that they dare move from the status quo to join the leader in their Vision.

Early Adopters and/or Rebels – These people are itching for a change from the current status. They have little to no engagement with the status quo. Once they notice the Second Man In join the Leader, they are quick to jump on board.

---

[30] Krug, Doug and Oakley, Ed. *Enlightened Leadership: Getting to the Heart of Change.* 1994. Fireside Books by Simon and Schuster. New York, NY.

The Majority or Herd – This is the most common type of person found in a group, the people that make up the median of a bell-shaped curve. Their importance is found in the sheer number of people that they represent. They are momentum shifters.

Late Adopters or Luddites – These people finally join the group only when they see that the pain of the change is less than the pain of the norm. Often, the group will either give them an ultimatum to conform or just replace them. Their numbers, however, are what give the group huge returns on investment opportunities. For a visual idea of moving the Herd, see the following illustration of 10 individuals taking the path of change at different stages.

If you have ten people in a group, and the Leader gets a vision, the group's return on investment (ROI) is very low. One way to look at it is, if one person believes in a vision and nine do not (1/9 = 0.11) then you only get an eleven-cent return on investment of a dollar of effort. Not a good return. This is why so many Leaders fail to get their good idea off the ground.

If the Leader can get one person, the Second Man In, to follow their lead — maybe based on past performances or friendship — then the return (2/8 = $0.25) grows, but is still well under a break-even return on investment for a dollar of effort. If the Second Man In has a measure of significance or credibility in the group's eyes, then very quickly you will attract the next players — the Early Adopters — into the group.

If the Leader and/or the Second Man In can persuade one or two Early Adopters to buy into the vision, the return more than doubles (4/6 = .66), but is still too low to have the company or idea thrive. Often, a Rebel will notice the activity going on and want to switch allegiance to the new group, just because it is new. Now the return on investment (5/5 =$1.00) starts to at least break even!

All this commotion attracts the eye of the Herd — a group of people willing to move but only if the move is seen as both advantageous and safe — and they want to see what others in the group are doing. The sixth person to join the group grows the return by 50% (6/4 =$1.50). The seventh person to join increases the return (7/3 = $2.30), and the eighth person jumps the return all the way to $4.00 (8/2 = $4.00).

Finally, the Late Adopters join in the vision and more than double the return on investment (9/1 = $9.00). Often this phenomenon is caused by three factors:

1. The Late Adopter quits or is fired and a better-suited person is hired for the new vision.

2. Economies of scale drive down the company's costs.

3. The increased size of the company attracts rebates and concessions from suppliers.

If you combine the two forces, Theater of the Mind and the return possibilities of Net Forward Energy, you can see the potential power of one individual with a believable Vision and the keystone player of the Second Man In. My hope is that I might get to play a key role of Second Man In for several more times in my life. I have worked at being an integral part of building a Parkinson's Pointe resource center in Denver, Colorado that would serve the needs of the growing PD community. If we create the right Vision, for the right reasons, our model in Denver could be duplicated around the country or the world.

The overarching goal of wanting to make a contribution through the empowerment of a group of people toward a S.M.A.R.T. vision is what my life focus has always been about.

What about you? Do you have a Vision? Which role do you play in your groups? What plays in the Theater of Your Mind? How much of a return on investment do you produce in your life? Uncovering the answers to all these questions can move you towards living a significant life!

RISE POINT:
PREPARATION FOR GROUP ADVANCEMENT

Chance favors the prepared mind. Increase the odds of your learning to thrive in life by creating a new Vision for your life with Parkinson's. Learn all you can to positively influence your life for the betterment of yourself and those around you. What type of person do you think you are in a group that is pursuing a Vision?

VANTAGE POINT:

MARK TOMKO,
OWNER OF METCO LANDSCAPE, INC.

I met Greg in the middle of 1991 at a business meeting — set up to discuss our growth — as we were a small, unorthodox landscape company filling a unique niche. Greg worked for a wholesale distributor of irrigation materials, Turf Irrigation Supply, from which we bought most of the materials for our projects. The seasonality of the landscape industry in Colorado makes it very difficult to manage cash flow going into the winter months. My meeting with Greg was designed to ensure that Metco would have a strong financial plan to carry us through the winter season. In doing so, we developed a great business relationship and friendship.

Metco continued to struggle with cash flow and productivity issues until 2001. We then asked Greg to join our fledgling organization to help set up internal business systems to increase our productivity. In 2002, we developed a number of key processes and procedures that helped drive a spurt in both sales and profitability. Greg continued to develop systems for us until 2007, the start of the Great Recession when — for career reasons — Greg needed to move on.

Using the knowledge we gained from Greg's systems, we actually thrived during the recession and came out of it in very healthy, debt-free form. As the economy recovered from 2011 to 2015, we once again grew very quickly and profitably.

I learned of Greg's diagnosis with Parkinson's disease in the middle of 2011. I did not see him often as he was working for another distributorship. When I became aware he was available for employment, I immediately rehired Greg in early 2016. Our growth was exploding and we needed to continue to refine and grow our systems on our quest to hit $50M in revenue as the largest landscaper in Colorado. Greg was instrumental in helping us achieve our goal. We indeed reached more than $50M in revenue by the time I was 55-years-old. After the Great Recession set-back, we recovered and in 2018, had more than $60M in revenue at an unprecedented net profit.

When Greg rejoined our firm in 2016, he still appeared to be in fairly good health and was handling his Parkinson's symptoms noticeably well. Then he received the news he had Prostate Cancer. Once again, a massive challenge came his way. He has a very strong faith and his disciplined life allowed him to attack the cancer to win that battle quickly.

Greg never complained nor whined, and he maintained his strong work ethic the entire time. He continued to provide important value to our firm as he assisted us with improving our hiring and purchasing agendas. Greg also helped with our annual strategic forum for the company by both planning and facilitating the event. Greg was able to stay focused and effective during these times. However, during the 2018 season I noticed his fatigue was increasing.

The key point to understand from our experiences is that people with Parkinson's can lead very active and fulfilling lives. Greg is a champion role model for Parkinson's, and with his regimented lifestyle of disciplined exercise and diet he managed his symptoms and surroundings very well.

Where there is no revelation, people cast off restraint;
but blessed is the one who heeds wisdom's instruction.
Proverbs 29:18

CHAPTER 16

STANDING IN THE GAP

REBUILDING SIGNIFICANCE PIECE-BY-PIECE

Atomic Events affect our existence in colossal, as well as molecular ways. By their very nature they impose lifelong impacts despite our best efforts to mitigate their effects. Most things in our normal lives have short term impacts because the negative effects typically wear off within a year or so. We talked about this in the different phases of Residual Uncertainty in *Chapter Seven*. You can overcome or work around normal life changes. Many people have gone through the same type of life changes before we experienced them. These common changes often sort themselves out anyway. It's just not the same with Atomic Events, where the repercussions of fallout appear interminable. I will never live another day of my life without Parkinson's disease nor the negative effects on my family and myself.

This awareness causes me to increase my focus on time management and accomplishing the key points or events on the bucket list of my life. In *Chapter Five*, I introduced the concept of being an On-Purpose Person by playing out the seeded tournaments of eight different roles in your life. Each role eventually crowned a champion task or item. You will recall that the really interesting tournament to play is the "Tournament of Champions". Every item in this bracket is a top priority in some sphere of your life, but there can only be one true champion for you. You probably also remember that the winner of my "Tournament of Champions" was creating a Parkinson's Community center called Parkinson's Pointe.

I wrote about changing paradigms in *Chapter Eleven*. As I look out over the rest of my life, I see a need to incorporate Parkinson's into building a legacy that will outlive me. I have mentioned how my faith gives me hope that someday I will be in Heaven for eternity with a perfect body. But what about my next possible 15 years here on earth?

I am writing this chapter just prior to my 64th birthday. While only God knows how much longer I will live, I know that I need to find a vision to pour my life into that will outlive my own efforts and have a positive impact on other people's lives. Psalm 39:4 *says, Lord, make me to know my life's end, and what is the measure of my days, that I may know how frail I am.*

MODEL:
ESTABLISHING NEW HABITS

I first read Mr. Covey's book, *The Seven Habits of Highly Effective People*[31] sometime in the 1990's as part of a time management seminar. The seven habits are just as effective today — if you implement them in your life — as they were over 30 years ago. The habits are:

---

[31] Covey, Stephen. *7 Habits of Highly Effective People: Powerful Lessons in Personal Change.* 1990. Simon and Schuster.

1. Be Proactive – Use an Internal Locus of Control. Choose your response to any stimuli. Be a "Response-Able" person.
2. Begin with the End in Mind – The Leadership Habit. This is what leaders do. They create the Vision for everyone to follow.
3. Put First Things First – The Management Habit. Chart the course of your Vision. Count the Cost of your Vision. Organize systems into a flow.
4. Seek First to Understand, Before being Understood – Learn to see things from other people's perspective. Good Communication is Covenantal rather than Contractual.
5. Think Win-Win – Never settle for bad negotiations. Always look at what the other person's interest is.
6. Synergize – Seek to make 2 + 2 = 6 in your life. Play to your strengths. Surround yourself with others who are strong in your weak areas.
7. Sharpen the Saw Regularly – Keep learning new things. Exercise your mind and body. Take the time to recharge your batteries.

To create a new habit in your life, you need three things added together:

1. Knowledge – Knowing what to do
2. Skill – Knowing how to do it
3. Aptitude – Desiring to do it

Hopefully, this book has given you the first two parts of this equation. Only you can influence the third aspect. Remember, if you practice this formula for 21 days and beyond, you will have a great chance of developing the habit(s) of your choice.

Applying the Seven Habits to my life, I have come up with the vision to help build a Parkinson's Community Center, called Parkinson's Pointe. My definition of vision is, "The ability to think about or plan events which lead to an imagined future or potential outcome". I have used this in my business career by creating and producing visionary business programs in my industry (Maxicom, Dividend Dollars, The Select Contractor, among others) which are still actively used today.

At a recent retirement party of a friend in the industry, I was approached by two different people who were customers of mine in a past employment situation. They both wanted me to know that each of them felt the visionary business programs I developed had positively changed the course of success their businesses enjoyed. This in turn changed the course of their personal lives for the better. Few people get the chance to hear this type of appreciation during their careers! I believe God has other plans for my energies now, which could have a larger and longer lasting impact on other people's lives.

There are thousands of people living in Colorado (over a million in the US) who have been diagnosed with Parkinson's Disease. They come in all ethnicities, genders, shapes, and socio-economic arenas. They have all heard the words, "You have Parkinson's Disease." and felt like the walls of their lives had been torn down.

The biblical Old Testament Governor of Persian Judea, Nehemiah,[32] was faced with the same daunting scenario when he wanted to return to Jerusalem and rebuild the walls (Habit #2) of the city after the Babylonians had destroyed Jerusalem in 586 B.C. Nehemiah had to approach (Habit #1) King Cyrus the Great to ask for permission to return to Jerusalem with enough resources (Habit #3) to rebuild the walls, after two previous attempts from other people had failed to do this. Nehemiah faced great adversity (Habit #4) from both his own countrymen and jealous outside influences. He developed a plan to have each person work on rebuilding the wall directly in front of their home (Habit #5) by supplying the building materials and the protection from Jerusalem's enemies while the people worked furiously (Habit #6). What others could not get done in 13 years of effort, Nehemiah accomplished in 52 days, because he utilized the power of Net Forward Energy. He got everyone on board with the Vision of rebuilding the wall, for protecting their own homes (Habit#7) and their close neighbors.

Parkinson's is a "Shaking Tsunami" which is about to hit the fastest growing segment of our population, those who are +65-years-old and

---

[32] *Nehemiah*, Chapters 2-14.

over. I discussed earlier that I share a dream (Second Man In) with other Parkinson's community leaders about developing and establishing Parkinson's Pointe, a one-of-a-kind community center for people with Parkinson's Disease in Colorado. This facility would be a place devoted to programs designed to help people with neurological movement disorders. Persons with PD — and their caregivers — would have a single location devoted to supplying educational seminars, exercise, nutrition, physical therapy, research study participation, and support groups. Nothing like this exists today but it will in the future!

I am currently working with several other people to start a Board of Directors who would oversee the creation, completion, and implementation of this dream. Our dream requires effort and substance to become a reality against the obstacles that will fall in front of us. The starter list of items to accomplish this goal includes: attract the proper personnel, communicate with the existing Parkinson's community segments regarding what we are trying to accomplish, find a location, obtain insurance, and pass appropriate licensing requirements.

Start-up funding at the early stages of a project is critical to amass even before you can apply for additional grants and foundation funding. I am asking for your help in realizing the dream of creating Parkinson's Pointe for the thousands of people in Colorado who will hear the words, "You have Parkinson's Disease." Over the coming years. I have a goal to raise $52,000.00 in seed capital to help fund all the initial costs of creating Parkinson's Pointe. Will you "stand in the gap of the wall" with me? Whether you know someone with Parkinson's, or would like to help in honor of a loved one who has already passed away from PD, this would be a monumental project to help achieve. Your assistance will go a long way in helping a growing number of people to learn to thrive in their lives despite having encountered a severe Atomic Event.

For more information on this important, project please visit:

www.parkinsonspointe.org

RISE POINT:
IDENTIFY YOUR SIGNIFICANT PURPOSE

What project or purpose do you want to pour your life into? Reading, learning, and practicing the *Seven Habits of Highly Effective People* is a great place to start. Seek out someone who can help you with the Knowledge and Skills of whatever habit you want to develop. You, and you alone, can supply the aptitude! What "wall" in your life do you need to have others help "stand in the gap" for and rebuild to make your life significant?

VANTAGE POINT:

SCOTT ABEL,
FRIEND

In the five years I've known Greg, he has always had Parkinson's Disease. However, I have never thought of him as, "Oh, my friend with Parkinson's". Right off the bat, I've seen my dear friend practice what he preaches. He asks others who know him well for feedback on their impression of how he is doing regarding his symptoms and insights. By doing this, he applies Habit #4 (Seek First to Understand) so this experience becomes part of building Habit #5 (Win-Win).

When I think of Greg and what defines him and his ability to "stand in the gap", it has always been his faith in God first. From there, being a devoted husband second, a caring father and an engaged grandfather third. He also maintains his awesome sense of humor, his disciplined regimen, his business know how, and his willingness to use these things in all facets of his life to help those around him — including dealing with Parkinson's Disease.

In my view, the definition of "stand in the gap" is to expose one's self for the protection of someone or something; to make defense against any assailing danger; and to take the place of a fallen defender or supporter.

Greg truly is doing this by living with intention for sharing the love of Jesus through his daily interaction, yet also by sharing his experiences overcoming this terrible disease, Parkinson's. He is honest, vulnerable, and living with faith-based intention. My life is better as I'm able to call Greg, "my friend". Many others will be better off through his vision of a fruitful life with his faith in God as the foundation, which he shares so candidly and vividly in this book.

God looks down from heaven on all mankind to see
if there are any who understand, any who seek God.
Psalm 53:2

CHAPTER 17

RISING ABOVE PARKINSON'S

LIFE IS AN OCCASION; RISE TO IT!

Writing this book has been an eye-opening experience. Few people get to hear the comments and thoughts of their loved ones and family expressed in the ways which I have been able to read in the VANTAGE POINT sections of this book. To me, it is almost worth having Parkinson's just to get to read through them!

Practice What You Preach
Towards the end of writing this book, another Atomic Event hit my life. My wife and I recently retired and had thoughts of finding a second beach home somewhere in the Gulf Coast states region. We planned a three month "walk about" to have extended stays in places we were considering, including South Padre Island, Texas; Galveston, Texas; MiraMar Beach, Florida; the "30-A" Highway area of Florida; and the Gulf Shores area of Alabama. We wanted to get a feel for each area and where we might invest in a warm home. Very On-Purpose of me, right?

Unfortunately, half way through our already paid for destination travels, I got a frantic call from my wife telling me our youngest daughter was in intensive care, having liver issues due to pregnancy (27 weeks). She was hospitalized back in Colorado Springs, Colorado, and was scheduled to have an emergency C-section in less than two days (Crisis change). We quickly assessed the situation.

First, we made phone calls to friends, Bible study groups, and church people asking for prayers for both my daughter and her child. Second, we quickly decided to cancel the rest of our trip and drive to Dallas, Texas where our middle daughter was attending a convention. She could drive our vehicle back to Colorado after her convention, so my wife and I could immediately fly home to Colorado from Dallas. We arrived at Denver International Airport just as a snowstorm was hitting the metro area. Due to the storm, it took us two hours longer than planned to get to our daughter in Colorado Springs. She had her C-section early the next morning. We were living the roller-coaster ride of having such a premature grandbaby. One second things were looking bright for her, and the next second another alarm would go off on one of the many machines she was hooked up to which monitored all her vital signs. I am happy to tell you that on January 22nd, 2020 we got to bring our little miracle, Emma, home. She is doing fine and it appears that she should be able to grow up healthy and live a normal life.

By implementing a number of the models I have shared in this book, we were able to reasonably react to (Internal Locus of Control) a potential deadly situation. Our prayers and intentions were that we could affect this situation in a positive way, turning a potential tragedy into a hard-won family story to be retold with joy at future holiday dinners for generations to come.

I would like to leave you with one last acronym to help you remember — in critical times when your thinking may be rushed or clouded — how to handle the Atomic Events which will happen in your life:

P – Power of Planning. Do not let Parkinson's just happen to you. Building a response support team is good, but already having a plan of attack (Noah Principle) is even better. Good plans start with a vision of where you want to go (50/50 Vision), and then are adaptable enough to handle uncontrollable Residual Uncertainty events popping up in your life. Be On Purpose about what Roles (Life Functions) you need to cover and don't be afraid to prioritize them ahead of time, so you know just what to do in an Atomic Event attack.

A – Atomic Events. These happen to everyone and change your normal life for the rest of your life. Often, F.E.A.R. (Future Expectations Appear Real) plays with your mind and it can create an unintended negative influence. One thing you can control is your Attitude — as Victor Frankl pointed out — you can uniquely choose your response to any negative stimuli (Response-Ability). All situations are constantly changing (Creative Destruction). You can never eliminate all uncertainty (Theory of Residual Uncertainty), but you can think through the situation and try to break down overwhelming problems into smaller parts to solve them one piece at a time.

R – Resources. Find them ahead of time, use them, and become one for others! Think about who might be on your support team. Look to develop a support system that covers most of the details that are now a part of your life. Check out various associations, specialty groups, and university study opportunities. Get involved. Help dictate the outcome of your story.

K – Kinder person. Try to find the things about life with Parkinson's Disease that might introduce you to new and better ways of thinking or acting. My family says I am a much kinder, gentler person now that I have Parkinson's. Look on the bright side of things. I have participated in over 30 different studies since I was diagnosed. Often, I will receive a small stipend to cover my time and travel. I started to put all that money in a 529 College Saving Fund for my grandchildren. I have raised over $5K since my diagnosis that might help put my grandchildren through the school of their choice. They say, "What goes around comes around".

I – Internal Locus of Control. Allows you to feel like you can have an influence on or help dictate an outcome in any situation. Just because you now have to deal with some Atomic Event in your life doesn't mean that you cannot learn new things or accomplish new goals. I have now climbed 10 mountains in Colorado more than 14,000' tall. I have found an artistic side of me that I never knew existed (see poem in *Chapter One*). You cannot manage something you do not measure. Take a look at starting your own yearly Life Assessment sheet and chart the Factors you deem important to your journey.

N – Neuroplasticity. The ability of your brain and body to alter or modify PD affected functioning to account for the loss of previously normal functioning. Parkinson's is constantly trying to take away our balance and make us stiff as a board. Yoga or Ti Chi are two different activities you can employ to re-learn balance every day. One part of your brain can be learning new tricks of the trade about balance as another part is losing it. Exercise is the great Elixir! There are many benefits to starting and maintaining an effective exercise program, especially one designed by a competent physical therapist. Set realistic goals and just do it!

S – Square Model. Looking at a big problem as a series of smaller problems (30 squares) to solve is a great way to look at figuring out how to live your new, post-Atomic Event life. Look to solve as many of the small, individual boxes (problems) as you can. This will help make the big problem box easier to overcome. Seek help and ideas from your support group for answers.

O – Ownership. One of the key parts of the C.O.O.R.E. model tells us that we can look at any problem and ascertain how much we can look at our own behavior as the source of the issue. Smoking cigarettes often leads to lung cancer. Whereas, colon cancer happens more by chance but does have a genetic predisposition. If it runs in your family, you should definitely take the proper precautions. As a Parkie, you are not a victim or defective. You have a disease, but you can control how you respond to Parkinson's symptoms in your life.

N – Noah Principle. This states it is not your ability to predict rain that counts, but rather your ability to have built an ark before the deluge begins (Atomic Event). Using the talents given you, take a look at your strengths and prepare for rain in your life. My daughter who had our premature granddaughter is a very social being. Because she was already active in MOPS groups and a church family, we started getting dinners brought to the house, a Go Fund Me account was set up to help defer medical costs, and offers came in to do the housework (that actually is my job!) within hours of her being admitted to the hospital.

S – S.M.A.R.T. Goals. These should be in everyone's life. An objective in life, without goals, is merely a dream. Giving yourself goals to achieve (climb a 14,000' mountain yearly) is important for a brighter outlook. It sets you up for preparation, resource gathering, and a nice shot of serotonin once you purposefully complete your goal. Be sure to be as specific and realistic as you can be about achieving your goal on a timely basis. Look to find people with a positive influence in your life and be one for someone else.

I wish you good luck — preparation running into opportunity — and God's speed in your life.

RISE POINT:
SIGNIFICANCE GIVES OTHERS HOPE

My wish for your life is that — in some meaningful way — this book has helped ignite a flame of passion in you to live a life of significance. I hope and pray you will have an impact on the lives of people around you while making the world a better place to live. The mantra of my life is:

"Success in life is a journey, not a destination.
Significance in life is a gift to others as it brings hope.
Life is an occasion; RISE to it!"

The secret things belong to the Lord our God,
but the things revealed belong to us and to our children forever,
that we may follow all the words of this law.
Deuteronomy 29:29

ENDNOTES

A. BETTER SLEEP

B. FACIAL EXERCISES

C. HOME REMEDY RECIPES

D. PARKINSON'S DISEASE INFORMATION

E. ORGANIZATIONS

F. MAKE TEN SOLUTION

A. BETTER SLEEP

[Excerpted from Holistic Brain Wellness © 2011 Monique L. Giroux, MD. Author of Optimal Health with Parkinson's Disease; A Guide to Integrating Lifestyle, Alternative, and Conventional Medicine. 2015. Demos Health.]

Make a commitment to better sleep by addressing the following:

Create A Sleepful Surrounding

- If you or your bed partner is snoring, kicking, or active in sleep, further medical evaluation may be needed.
- Keep your room dark while sleeping; dim the lights 1-2 hours before your regular bedtime.
- Keep your bedroom cool and quiet; use soft background noise if needed to block out street or household noise.
- Pets may be cute and cuddly but are they keeping you awake?
- Play quiet, relaxing music.
- Quiet the mind. A guided imagery CD can be played at the bedside; http://www.healthjourneys.com by Bellaruth Naparastek.
- Remove the TV (and other screens) from your bedroom.

Food and Supplements

- Avoid alcohol and nicotine at night.
- Avoid large, heavy evening meals. Opt for light snacks. Eat snacks high in complex carbohydrates such as whole grain bread, oats. This helps the transport of tryptophan (precursor to melatonin) into the brain.
- Avoid high sugar foods before bed.
- Consider taking Melatonin, which is a natural hormone that controls circadian changes or our internal sleep/wake cycle. Melatonin should be increased during dark hours. Talk to your doctor if you have breast or prostate cancer or are on blood thinners before using. 1-5 mg sustained release. Sublingual may offer more predictable absorption.

- Drink fluids before 6:00 pm and not later if you wake up frequently to urinate.
- Reduce caffeine beverages to 8 oz. in morning only; avoid consuming later in day or evening, including chocolate, coffee, soda, and tea.
- Valerian Root, Lemon Balm, or Chamomile as a soothing tea can be used in your 'relaxing practice'.

Physical Body
Review treatments and medicines for symptoms that may awaken you.

- Breathing problems
- Muscle spasms
- Pain
- Sleep apnea
- Sudden movements

Sleep Comfort

- Mattress – If it is a problem, can it be modified or replaced?
- Room temperature – A cooler room temperature (68°F) helps with sleep.
- Muscle discomfort, tremor, or stiffness can awaken you – there may be prescription drug changes that can help if this is related to your condition. Talk with your doctor about your symptoms.

Sleep Schedule

- Avoid clock watching bed positions; turn the display away from your sight.
- Begin a sleep ritual two hours before bed.
- Dim lights at night to reduce sensory stimulation, and slow down.
- If not sleeping, get out of bed for 20 minutes then return.
- Quiet the mind with mind-body techniques.
- Restful practice: gentle stretching, music, warm bath, yoga.
- Use bed only for sleep and sex, not other activities.

B. FACIAL EXERCISES

- Chew with lips closed
- Curl lips into mouth
- Frown
- Grin as wide as possible
- Make expression as if you smell something terrible
- Make expression of surprise, with open mouth
- Open mouth wide and move jaw back and forth
- Pucker lips in a kiss
- Puff cheeks with air
- Smile with lips closed, teeth together
- Turn bottom lip over

C. HOME REMEDY RECIPES

For Bowel Regularity – Compliments of our fellow Parkies!

#1 - Fruit Paste

Ingredients

- 1 lb. pitted prunes
- 1 lb. raisins
- 1 lb. figs 3%
- 4, 1 oz. packages Senna tea (found in health food stores)
- 1 c. brown sugar
- 1 c. lemon juice

Preparation, Storage, and Use

1. Prepare tea: Use about 3 c. boiling water to one package of tea.
2. Steep for 5 minutes. Strain tea to remove leaves.
3. Add only 2 cups of tea to a large pot.
4. Add fruit.
5. Boil tea and fruit for 5 minutes.
6. Remove from heat.
7. Add sugar and lemon juice.
8. Cool.
9. Use a food processor or blender to turn the mixture into smooth paste.
10. Place in glass jars or Tupperware containers and put in the freezer.
11. Paste will not freeze and will keep for a long time.
12. Use 1 or 2 tablespoons daily on crackers, toast, or cereal.
13. Take as little or as much as necessary to stimulate at least one bowel movement a day, but not so much as to cause diarrhea.
14. If #1 seems too much trouble, try Recipe #2

#2 - Rancho Sauce
(Don't ask about the name!)

Ingredients:

- 1 cup applesauce
- 1 cup oat bran or unprocessed wheat bran
- 1 cup of prune juice

Preparation, Storage, and Use:

1. Mix ingredients together.
2. Begin with 1-2 tablespoons each evening mixed with or followed by one 6-8 oz. cup of water or juice.
3. This should help to soften and regulate your bowel movements within 2 weeks.
4. If no change occurs, slowly increase serving to 3-4 tablespoons.
5. This may be stored in your refrigerator or freezer.
6. 1-2 tablespoon servings may be frozen in sectioned ice cube trays or in foam plastic egg cartons and thawed as needed.
7. If #2 seems too much trouble, try Recipe #3 (my personal favorite!)

#3 - Take a Break!
(Way easy!)

Ingredients:

- 1 package of Metamucil multigrain wafer (Apple Crisp or Cinnamon Spice; sold in grocery stores)
- 1 cup of your favorite tea

Preparation, Storage, and Use:

1. Take a tea and "cookie" break mid-afternoon.
2. You can always add a mid-morning break for more relief.
3. The wafers come individually wrapped, making them great for traveling.

D. PARKINSON'S DISEASE INFORMATION

From the National Institute of Neurological Disorders and Stroke

(Excerpted and retrieved 1.22.20 from https://www.ninds.nih.gov/ Disorders/All-Disorders/Parkinsons-Disease-Information-Page)

Definition of Parkinson's Disease

Parkinson's Disease (PD) belongs to a group of conditions called motor system disorders, which are the result of the loss of dopamine-producing brain cells. The four primary symptoms of PD are tremor, or trembling in hands, arms, legs, jaw, and face; rigidity, or stiffness of the limbs and trunk; bradykinesia, or slowness of movement; and postural instability, or impaired balance and coordination.

As these symptoms become more pronounced, patients may have difficulty walking, talking, or completing other simple tasks. PD usually affects people over the age of 60. Early symptoms of PD are subtle and occur gradually. In some people the disease progresses more quickly than in others. As the disease progresses, the shaking, or tremor, which affects the majority of people with PD may begin to interfere with daily activities.

Other symptoms may include depression and other emotional changes; difficulty in swallowing, chewing, and speaking; urinary problems or constipation; skin problems; and sleep disruptions. There are currently no blood or laboratory tests that have been proven to help in diagnosing sporadic PD. Therefore, the diagnosis is based on medical history and a neurological examination. The disease can be difficult to diagnose accurately. Doctors may sometimes request brain scans or laboratory tests in order to rule out other diseases.

Treatment of Parkinson's Disease

At present, there is no cure for PD, but a variety of medications provide dramatic relief from the symptoms. Usually, affected individuals are given levodopa combined with carbidopa. Carbidopa delays the conversion of levodopa into dopamine until it reaches the brain. Nerve cells can use levodopa to make dopamine and replenish the brain's dwindling supply. Although levodopa helps at least three-quarters of Parkinsonian cases, not all symptoms respond equally to the drug. Bradykinesia and rigidity respond best, while tremor may be only marginally reduced. Problems with balance and other symptoms may not be alleviated at all. Anticholinergics may help control tremor and rigidity.

Other drugs, such as bromocriptine, pramipexole, and ropinirole, mimic the role of dopamine in the brain, causing the neurons to react as they would to dopamine. An antiviral drug, amantadine, also appears to reduce symptoms. In May 2006, the Food and Drug Administration approved rasagiline to be used along with levodopa for patients with advanced PD or as a single-drug treatment for early PD. The FDA also has approved safinamide tablets and istradefylline tablets as an add-on treatment for individuals with PD who are currently taking levodopa/carbidopa and experiencing "Off" episodes (when the person's medications are not working well, causing an increase in PD symptoms).

In some cases, surgery may be appropriate if the disease doesn't respond to drugs. A therapy called deep brain stimulation (DBS) has now been approved by the U.S. Food and Drug Administration. In DBS, electrodes are implanted into the brain and connected to a small electrical device called a pulse generator that can be externally programmed. DBS can reduce the need for levodopa and related drugs, which in turn decreases the involuntary movements called dyskinesias that are a common side effect of levodopa. It also helps to alleviate fluctuations of symptoms and to reduce tremors, slowness of movements, and gait problems. DBS requires careful programming of the stimulator device in order to work correctly.

Prognosis of Parkinson's Disease

PD is both chronic, meaning it persists over a long period of time, and progressive, meaning its symptoms grow worse over time. Although some people become severely disabled, others experience only minor motor disruptions. Tremor is the major symptom for some individuals, while for others tremor is only a minor complaint and other symptoms are more troublesome. It is currently not possible to predict which symptoms will affect an individual, and the intensity of the symptoms also varies from person to person.

What research is being done regarding Parkinson's Disease?

Current research programs funded by the National Institute of Neurological Disorders and Stroke are using animal models to study how the disease progresses with drug therapies. Scientists looking for the cause of PD continue to search for possible environmental factors, such as toxins, that may trigger the disorder, and study genetic factors to determine how defective genes play a role. Other scientists are working to develop new protective drugs that can delay, prevent, or reverse the disease.

E. ORGANIZATIONS

From the National Institute of Neurological Disorders and Stroke

(Excerpted and retrieved 1.22.20 from https://www.ninds.nih.gov/ Disorders/All-Disorders/Parkinsons-Disease-Information-Page)

American Parkinson Disease Association
135 Parkinson Avenue
Staten Island, NY   10305-1425
apda@apdaparkinson.org
http://www.apdaparkinson.org
718-981-8001; 800-223-2732; 877-223-3801 (Young Onset Center)

Bachmann-Strauss Dystonia & Parkinson Foundation
P.O. Box 38016
Albany, NY   12203
info@bsdpf.org
http://www.dystonia-parkinsons.org
212-509-0995

Davis Phinney Foundation
357 S. McCaslin Boulevard, Suite 105
Louisville, CO   80027
info@davisphinneyfoundation.org
https://www.davisphinneyfoundation.org
866-358-0285; 303-733-3340

Michael J. Fox Foundation for Parkinson's Research Grand Central Station
P.O. Box 4777
New York, NY   10163
https://www.michaeljfox.org/
212-509-0995

The Parkinson Alliance
P.O. Box 308
Kingston, NJ   08528-0308
http://www.parkinsonalliance.org
609-688-0870; 800-579-8440

Parkinson's Foundation
1359 Broadway, Suite 1509
New York, NY   10018
contact@parkinson.org
https://www.parkinson.org/
800-473-4636

Parkinson's Resource Organization
74-090 El Paseo, Suite 104
Palm Desert, CA   92260
info@parkinsonsresource.org
http://www.parkinsonsresource.org
760-773-5628; 877-775-4111; 877-775-4111

The Parkinson's Institute and Clinical Center
2500 Hospital Drive Building #0, Suite 1
Mountain View, CA   94040
info@thepi.org
http://www.thepi.org.
408-734-2800; 800-655-2273

F. MAKE TEN SOLUTION

Made in the USA
Columbia, SC
06 March 2022

57061235R10113